BIBLICAL BISHOPS
JAMES USSHER'S DEFENCE AND REFORM
OF ANGLICAN POLITY

PETER BLAIR

The Latimer Trust

ISBN 978-1-906327-73-6 Published by the Latimer Trust February 2022.

The Latimer Trust (formerly Latimer House, Oxford) is a conservative Evangelical research organisation within the Church of England, whose main aim is to promote the history and theology of Anglicanism as understood by those in the Reformed tradition. Interested readers are welcome to consult its website for further details of its many activities.

The Latimer Trust
London N14 4PS UK
Registered Charity: 1084337
Company Number: 4104465
Web: www.latimertrust.org
E-mail: administrator@latimertrust.org

As an introduction to the thought of Archbishop Ussher on the nature of the episcopacy, Peter Blair's work both informs and stimulates. In particular it challenges us to re-think the episcopacy as a biblical ministry. I warmly commend it.

Dr Peter Jensen, former Archbishop of Sydney

Amid the controversies of the seventeenth century, one moderate and comprehensive voice stands out -- that of Archbishop James Ussher. His proposals for bishops in a Reformed church failed to catch on at the time, but in our more ecumenical age they deserve to be heard again. Peter Blair has done this in a winsome way that may help us reassess and renew the episcopate for the global Church of tomorrow.

Gerald Bray is Director of Research for the Latimer Trust and Research Professor at Beeson Divinity School, Samford University, Birmingham, Alabama, USA

Revd Peter Blair clearly sets out that Archbishop Ussher was defining the office and role of a bishop, not in response to institutional requirements or ecclesiological distinctives, but first and fore mostly from his own close reading of Holy Scripture. Every faithful theologian, presbyter, and bishop must learn to navigate their own cultural moment while maintaining a robust confidence the goodness and sufficiency of God's Word. In this regard, Revd Blair ably and helpfully holds up Ussher as a model worth following today."

David Martin, Director of Irish Church Missions

Bishops (or overseers) are good for the church, but what type of bishops do we need today? Our inherited Anglican order requires urgent rethinking, and James Ussher is an excellent conversation partner, because he engaged in the same project in his generation. Archbishop Ussher – helpfully distilled here in brief by Peter Blair – takes us back to the Bible and the early Christians, to think again.

Andrew Atherstone, Latimer Research Fellow, Wycliffe Hall, Oxford

CONTENTS

PREFACE

Evangelical Anglicans have in the past been woefully ignorant about the Biblical and historical basis for our church polity. This has not helped evangelical bishops understand their role biblically and theologically and has left us with often little more than pragmatic answers to questions of role and structure.

Shortly after my consecration, due to a prompt by a footnote in a book called 'Puritan Profiles', I discovered the influence of Archbishop James Ussher on the Westminster Divines. I went searching in the Lambeth Palace Library for his writing on Episcopacy. What I found was thrilling and convincing. Ussher as a Calvinist and Puritan sympathiser had placed the role of bishops not just as a post New Testament development (legitimate or otherwise) but as overlapping with the Apostolic era and found within the pages of the Bible itself (both in the Old and New Testament embryonically. I became a huge fan of his succinct and biblically convincing arguments. His was not novel reasoning but was perhaps the high-water mark of Reformed Anglican thinking on polity. What a treasure it was to discover! And how it made me think hard as well as wish that the king had accepted Ussher's suggestions for the reduction and reform of episcopacy. How it would perhaps have delivered us from modern day prelacy! I shared what I found in a St Antholin Lecture (reprinted by Latimer in 'Preachers, Pastors, and Ambassadors', 2011).

We owe a great debt of gratitude to Peter Blair for this dissertation, which has done a far more thorough job than I did to explain the historical background and nuances of Ussher's views. What he has written is very well researched but accessible, and raises all the right questions for us to profitably think through in the light of his exposition of Ussher's views. It is wonderful to see a new generation much more aware of our heritage, and Peter's work will undoubtedly help us further with this knowledge. There are excellent reasons for being a 'Reformed Anglican'- read on and discover!

Wallace Benn, Pentecost 2021

ABBREVIATIONS

ANF	*The Ante-Nicene Fathers,* ed. Alexander Roberts and James Donaldson, 9 vols., Buffalo and New York: Christian Literature Company, 1885–96.
NPNF 1/	*A Select Library of the Nicene and Post-Nicene Fathers of the Christian Church,* ed. Philip Schaff, 14 vols., Buffalo and New York: Christian Literature Company, 1886–90.
NPNF 2/	*A Select Library of the Nicene and Post-Nicene Fathers of the Christian Church, Second Series,* ed. Philip Schaff and Henry Wace, 14 vols., Buffalo and New York: Christian Literature Company, 1890–1900.
LEP	*Richard Hooker Of the Lawes of Ecclesiastical Polity: Introductions; Commentary, Preface and Books I–VIII,* eds. W. Speed Hill et al., 6 vols., Folger Library, New York: Center for Medieval and Early Renaissance Studies, 1993.
OB	'The Original of Bishops and Metropolitans (1644),' ed. Richard Snoddy, *James Ussher and a Reformed Episcopal Church: Sermons and Treatises on Ecclesiology,* Lincoln, NE: Davenant Press, 2018, 118–47.
PG	*Patrologia Graeca,* ed. J.-P. Migne, 161 vols., Paris, 1857–66.
PL	*Patrologia Latina,* ed. J.-P. Migne, 221 vols., Paris, 1844–64.
WCF	*The Westminster Confession of Faith: The Confession of Faith, The Larger and Shorter Catechism, The Sum of Saving Knowledge, The Directory for Public Worship & Other Associated Documents,* Edinburgh: Banner of Truth, 2018.
WJU	*The Whole Works of the Most Rev. James Ussher, D.D., Lord Bishop of Armagh, and Primate of All Ireland,* eds. Charles R. Elrington and J. H. Todd, 17 vols., Dublin: Hodges, Smith, & Co., 1829–64.

Conventions

When citing primary early modern sources, the original irregular spelling, punctuation and capitalisation has been preserved, aside from the modernisation of the letter 's'.

The terms Presbyterian and Puritan are capitalised throughout.

The word church will only be capitalised when used as a proper noun, i.e. the Church of England.

Although many early modern texts capitalise the entirety of their titles, only the first letter of each word, apart from prepositions and conjunctions, will be capitalised.

Acknowledgements

I am deeply grateful to the numerous people who made this study possible. First, I would like to thank Trevor Johnston, my trainer, rector and friend, who introduced me to the world of reformational Anglicanism, past and present. Secondly, I would like to thank everyone in the UK and Australia who prayerfully, financially and personally supported my studies at Moore Theological College, which enabled me to produce this work. Thirdly, I would like to thank Mark Earngey for his friendship and supervision of this project, as well as Mark Thompson and Peter Orr for their encouragements to not leave Ussher behind once college had finished. Fourthly, Daniel Ritchie, Wallace Benn and the wonderful people at Latimer Trust provided much needed feedback, and Caitlin Buick gave the manuscript a much-needed proofread. Any errors that remain are mine alone. Finally, I would like to thank my long-suffering wife, Jodie. She is God's greatest gift to me besides Christ. It is to her that I dedicate this work.

INTRODUCTION

The song remains the same

The seventeenth century was a tumultuous time for the Church of England. Theological division existed across the British Isles; questions concerning the authority of bishops, and even the validity of the office itself, abounded in major churches and evangelical seminaries. Much of this turbulence was fuelled by fellow reformed Christians abroad. Though separated by centuries, the problems with the Church of England in the 1600s were not so different to those emerging in many quarters of the Anglican communion today.

The presence of these questions and conflicts ought not to surprise the student of Scripture. Division existed even among the apostles: from multiple disputes about who was the greatest among them (Luke 9:46; 22:24) to repeated debates and disputes concerning Gentiles and the Old Testament law (Acts 15:7; Gal 2:11). After the ascension of Jesus, the apostles turned to the Scriptures themselves to answer these debates. At the Jerusalem Council, James appealed to the writings of the prophet Amos. In his rebuke of Peter, and the Galatian church which had fallen into the same error, Paul cites Genesis 15 – that Abraham was counted righteous because of his belief, not because of his works.

Following these apostolic examples, this booklet with return to the Scriptures to discern the question of whether bishops are in fact 'biblical'. However, we will not return to the Scriptures on our own. James Ussher (1581–1656), Archbishop of Armagh and Primate of All Ireland, will be our guide.

Why James Ussher? The good archbishop presents a curious case of reformed catholicity, remarkable in his day and in ours. Alan Ford, Ussher's most recent biographer, describes the archbishop as having a 'Janus-like quality'.[1] He was a staunch defender of episcopacy, yet was a friend of and admired by both Presbyterian and Congregational churchmen. He was a critic of royal tolerance, yet was a divine right

---

[1] Alan Ford, *James Ussher: Theology, History, and Politics in Early-Modern Ireland and England* (Oxford: Oxford University Press, 2007), 5, 231.

absolutist.[2] William Laud described him as a dear friend, yet his Irish Articles are considered to be a 'chief source' of the *Westminster Confession of Faith*.[3] He was on excellent terms with both Charles I and Oliver Cromwell. His bond with the latter was demonstrated at his death, when Cromwell insisted that the archbishop's funeral take place in Westminster Abbey, that it be funded by the state, and perhaps most notably, that it be granted permission to use the liturgy of the *Book of Common Prayer* – the only Prayer Book service to take place in the Abbey under the Protectorate.[4] Ussher, therefore, was no prelatical partisan. He was, and indeed remains, a fine example of Reformed Catholicism.

Ussher's Reformed Catholicity has been used to dispute the very existence of his own episcopal convictions. In the mid-twentieth century, the Irish historian A. F. S. Pearson coined the term 'prescopalian', not merely as a description of the Church of Ireland in the seventeenth century, but of Ussher's premeditated desire to combine the two forms of church government in the future.[5] More recently, Ussher has been charged with 'promoting presbyterian government.'[6] Was James Ussher attempting to presbyterianise episcopalianism? By examining Ussher's defence and suggested reform of the Church of England's ecclesiastical structures, this book will also seek to determine whether or not 'prescopalian' is a fitting title for Ussher's ecclesiastical intentions.

Before going any further, it is worth stating what this book is *not*. It is not a comprehensive defence of episcopalian government against Presbyterian or Congregational models. There are passages, positions, and persons that Ussher does not address. What this book attempts to

---

[2] Ford, *James Ussher,* 5, 230.
[3] Philip Schaff, *The Creeds of Christendom,* Bibliotheca symbolica ecclesiae universalis, 3 vols. (New York: Harper Longmans, 1919), 526; J. V. Fesko, *The Theology of the Westminster Standards* (Wheaton: Crossway, 2014), 60.
[4] Charles Elrington, 'The Life of James Ussher,' *WJU,* 1:279.
[5] Pearson combines the terms Presbyterian and Episcopalian in A. F. S. Pearson, 'Puritan and Presbyterian Settlements in Ireland 1560–1660' in *Presbyterian Origins in Ireland* (Belfast: Presbyterian Historical Society of Ireland, 1948), 5–8. Cited in Ford, *James Ussher,* 168–69. Eric Culbertson, *The Evangelical Roots of the Church of Ireland: James Ussher and the Irish Articles* (Lisburn, Northern Ireland: CIEF, 1999), 34.
[6] Coleman Ford, '"Everywhere, Always, By All": William Perkins and James Ussher on the Constructive Use of the Fathers,' *Puritan Reformed Journal* 2 (2015): 95.

provide is fuel for discussion surrounding the validity and nature of episcopal oversight from a biblical and historical perspective. In doing so, it hopes to present a fresh journey through Scripture and history, led by the erudite but often overlooked James Ussher.

The first chapter will begin with a brief biography of the archbishop, noting particularly the ecclesiastical influences impressed upon Ussher by his family and his Puritan education. It will then consider the ecclesiastical influence impressed by Ussher upon the Church of Ireland. Although Ussher enjoyed significant influence on English clergy following his move to England in 1640, chapter one will primarily consider his Irish influence, as it was the Church of Ireland that Pearson dubbed 'prescopalian'.

The next four chapters will focus on Ussher's two major works on ecclesiastical matters: chapters two, three and four will consider *The Original of Bishops and Metropolitans* (1644), within which Ussher outlines the biblical and historical case for episcopal oversight; chapter five will consider *The Reduction of Episcopacy* (1657) which proposed Ussher's focused plan to reduce the episcopate of the Church of England.

Although Ussher produced other ecclesiological works, this book will focus on these two texts for three reasons. First, *The Original* and *The Reduction* are exclusively ecclesiastical (dealing with the issue of church government and structure) – whereas the four sermons recently compiled by Richard Snoddy are primarily ecclesiological (dealing with eschatology, catholicity, the sacraments and ecumenism).[7] Secondly, these two texts are his longest and most direct treatment of episcopal oversight, dealing with both biblical and historical data (*The Original*), as well as outlining a practical, step-by-step guide for the reform of episcopacy in the seventeenth-century Church of England (*The Reduction*). Thirdly, both works were written towards the end of his life, after 40 years of ordained ministry and scholarship. As such, they offer the fullness of Ussher's position on the subject, representing a synthesis on his earlier, mainly historiographical writings on the topic of episcopacy. Such an assessment will go some way in determining whether Ussher's definition of episcopacy was a biblical form of church government, or whether it was a

---

[7] Richard Snoddy, ed., *James Ussher and a Reformed Episcopal Church: Sermons and Treatises in Ecclesiology* (Moscow, ID: Davenant Press, 2018), 1–117.

compromised concession on the road to a mixed 'prescopalian' ecclesiastical structure.

CHAPTER I

THE LIFE AND TIMES OF JAMES USSHER

Early life

The ecclesiastical tensions into which Ussher wrote *The Original* and *The Reduction* would have been familiar territory for the archbishop. Even in his youth, the Ussher family was torn by ecclesial divisions. Henry Ussher, his paternal uncle, was Archbishop of Armagh (1595–1615) and one of the founders of the then Puritan stronghold, Trinity College Dublin (TCD). His maternal uncle, Richard Stanihurst, was an Irish Catholic advocate on the continent, and his cousin, Henry Fitzsimon, was a Jesuit missionary in Ireland. His mother Margaret, despite raising her son as a protestant, converted to Roman Catholicism towards the end of her life. As well as providing an insight into the familial tensions of the Ussher family, these tensions capture the wider religious divisions present in seventeenth-century Ireland.

Education

In 1594, at the age of 13, Ussher entered TCD – one year after it had been established. Following the English undergraduate trivium of grammar, rhetoric and logic, Ussher would not formally study theology until he began his MA in 1598. Despite lacking any formal theological content, a reformed philosophy and epistemology guided Ussher's undergraduate studies, with the French Calvinist Pierre de la Ramée (Peter Ramus) dominating Ussher's student notebooks from that period.[8] Although Ramus was read widely across mainland Europe by Lutheran, Arminian and even Roman Catholic schools, his work was particularly associated with Calvinist Puritan institutions among the British Isles.[9] Compounding this Calvinist influence was the Presbyterian triumvirate of tutors at TCD: James Fullerton, James Hamilton and Walter Travers. Buick Knox, Ussher's twentieth-century biographer and Presbyterian minister, insists that Fullerton and Hamilton were no 'Presbyterian

---

[8] Ford, *James Ussher*, 39.
[9] J. S. Freedman, 'The Diffusion of the Writings of Peter Ramus in Central Europe c.1570–c.1630,' *Renaissance Quarterly* 46 (1993): 98–153.

propagandists' during their time in Dublin.[10] If Knox is correct about Fullerton and Hamilton, it is difficult to imagine that the same could be said of Travers. Before his appointment as Provost of TCD in 1594, Travers was famous for his public and robust criticism of episcopal polity which was propagated first in his work, *A Full and Plaine Declaration of Ecclesiastical Discipline out of the Word of God* (1574). Travers' opposition to episcopacy was reaffirmed in his infamous clash with Richard Hooker at the London Temple Church during the early 1580s, before he was forbidden to preach by Archbishop Whitgift in 1586.

Charles Elrington – Ussher's biographer and editor of his collected works – is reluctant to consider that the Puritanism of TCD's tutors had any lasting effect on the future archbishop.[11] For Elrington, the only significant influence he recognises is the development of Ussher's lifelong interest in the early church fathers. Summarising Ussher's education, Elrington writes that, 'Ussher, even at that early period, was impressed with the truth of Tertullian's maxim, "Verum quodcunque primum, adulterum quodcunque posterius."'[12] Elrington's reluctance to acknowledge a Presbyterian or Puritan influence may betray his own high church priorities more than Ussher's, in a phenomenon that Ford identifies as the 'subconscious temptation for biographers to mould [Ussher] to fit their own preferences or prejudices.'[13] Ford himself concludes that it is impossible to establish the degree of influence that Ussher's education had on his ecclesiological and ecclesiastical convictions.[14] Whilst the precise degree of influence may be impossible to establish with certainty, given the convictions of his tutors (particularly the verbose character of Travers), it is likely that Ussher would have been well aware of the arguments surrounding church government from an early age.

In 1600, following the award of his MA, Ussher was made a fellow of Trinity College Dublin. One year later, he was ordained both deacon and priest on Christmas Eve, 1601. At only 21, he was three years below the minimum age of ordination in the Church of Ireland. This breach of

---

[10] Buick Knox, *James Ussher: Archbishop of Armagh* (Cardiff: University of Wales Press, 1967), 16.

[11] Elrington and Todd, *The Whole Works*.

[12] Elrington, 'Life of James Ussher,' *WJU*, 1:9: 'Whatever comes first is true, whatever comes after is an adultery.'

[13] Ford, *James Ussher*, 5.

[14] Ford, *James Ussher*, 243.

order reveals the pressing need for protestant clergy in Roman Catholic-dominated Ireland. It also speaks of the high regard within which the young scholar was held by the church. It also may indicate a degree of nepotism, given that his own uncle Henry was the bishop who ordained him. For the next 20 years, the young Ussher enjoyed a prominent preaching ministry across Dublin alongside an acclaimed academic career. In recognition of his academic prowess, Ussher was appointed Vice-Chancellor of TCD. Shortly after, in 1615, Ussher spearheaded the Irish convocation's drawing-up of *The Irish Articles of Religion.*

Rigid precision: the Irish Articles

The *Irish Articles* include, with some minor alterations, 36 of the English Articles and all 9 of Whitgift's *Lambeth Articles* of 1595. Alongside the explicit predestinarianism of the *Lambeth Articles*, the *Irish Articles* are notable as the first English confessional document to articulate a twofold covenant theology. Covenant theology itself was not a new development in the theology of the English Reformation. The *Reformatio Legum Ecclesiasticarum,* produced a century earlier under the supervision of Archbishop Thomas Cranmer, articulated a covenantal doctrine of infant baptism.[15] Similarly, Thomas Rogers' 1587 commentary on the English *Thirty-Nine Articles of Religion* states that 'Children belong to the Kingdom of Heaven ... and are in the covenant; therefore the signe of the covenant is not to bee denied them.'[16] Although covenant theology was present at the earliest stages of the reformed Church of England, the twofold 'covenant of law and covenant of grace' of the *Irish Articles* was a more recent development, only beginning to emerge in England towards the end of the sixteenth century in the writings of Puritans such as Thomas Cartwright, Dudley Fenner and William Perkins.[17] The Church of Ireland's inclusion of this developed covenant theology moved it beyond the basic reformed theology of the Church of England's *Thirty-Nine Articles of Religion*, leaving some of Ussher's contemporaries to be

[15] Thomas Cranmer, 'Reformatio Legum Ecclesiasticarum' in Gerald Bray, ed., *Tudor Church Reform: The Henrician Canons of 1535 and the Reformatio Legum Ecclesiasticarum* (Woodbridge, Suffolk: Boydell & Brewer, 2000), 201.
[16] Thomas Rogers, *The English Creede* (London: n.p., 1587), 49.
[17] Michael McGiffert, 'Grace and Works: The Rise and Division of Covenant Divinity in Elizabethan Puritanism,' *Harvard Theological Review* 75 (1982): 463–502. See also Harrison Perkins, *Catholicity and the Covenant of Works: James Ussher and the Reformed Tradition* (Oxford: OUP, 2020).

concerned that the entire Church of Ireland had become a Puritan church.[18] While the presence of a twofold covenant theology is insufficient to categorise an entire church as Puritan, the speed with which the *Irish Articles* picked up this recent theological development indicates the significant influence that English Puritanism had on the Irish church.

Alongside their covenantal theology, the absence of ecclesiastical content in the *Irish Articles* also led to them being criticised as Puritan, even in Ussher's own lifetime. One such critic was the Laudian polemicist Peter Heylyn. Both a priest and a historian, Heylyn embodied what Peter Lake has identified as the emerging 'avante-guarde conformism' of the seventeenth century.[19] Heylyn condemned the 'Calvinian rigors' of the *Irish Articles,* evidenced in their 'silence concerning the consecration of arch-bishops and bishops (expresly justified and avowed in the English book), as if they were not a distinct order from the common presbyters.'[20] Heylyn's argument seems to be amplified by their solitary reference to an episcopal figure: the Bishop of Rome, whose authority is denounced as a 'usurped power, contrary to the Scriptures and word of God, and contrary to the example of the Primitive Church.'[21] Does the silence of the *Irish Articles* on the subject of episcopacy suggest a latent 'prescopalianism' in the young Ussher?

The 'rigid precision' of the *Irish Articles* – evidenced in their predestinarianism, covenant theology and their silence on episcopacy – has been lamented by Elrington as 'most injurious to the progress of true religion', arguably distancing the Irish church from its sister across the

---

[18] Gribben, Crawford. *The Irish Puritans: James Ussher and the Reformation of the Church* (Darlington, England: Evangelical Press, 2003), 39.

[19] Peter Lake, 'Lancelot Andrews, John Buckeridge and avant guarde conformity at the court of James I' in Linda L. Peck, ed., *The Mental World of the Jacobean Court* (Cambridge: CUP, 1991), 113–133.

[20] Peter Heylyn, *Aerius Redivivus, or, the History of the Presbyterians. Containing the Beginnings, Progresse, and Successes of that Active Sect. Their Oppositions to Monarchical and Episcopal Government. Their Innovations in the Church: and their Imbroilments of the Kingdoms and Eftares of Christendom in the pursuit of their Designs. From the Year 1537 to the Year 1647.* (Oxford: n.p., 1670), 394.

[21] Article 79, 'The Irish Articles of Religion' in Schaff, *The Creeds of Christendom*, d., 540. Capitalisation original.

Channel.[22] However, an analysis of the content of the *Irish Articles* compared with the confessional documents of the Church of England at that time suggests otherwise. Thirty-six of the *Thirty-Nine Articles* are adopted in whole or in part, with the additional content drawn almost exclusively from the *Lambeth Articles* and *Book of Homilies*.[23] As both Schaff and Fesko acknowledge, the *Irish Articles* went on to become a 'chief source' of the Westminster Confession.[24] However, it would be a chronological error to identify a latent Presbyterianism in the *Articles* themselves. The *Articles* may have been at odds with the theological and ecclesiastical emphases of Elrington and Heylyn's churchmanship. However, rather than separating the Irish church from the Church of England, the *Articles* sought to consolidate the Irish church with the theology of the English Church in the seventeenth century.

Bishop, then archbishop

Two years before the Irish convocation drew up the *Irish Articles*, Ussher published his first work, *De Christianorum Ecclesiarum Successione et Statu historica Explicatio* (1613), charting the historical succession and continuation of the Christian church from the first-century apostles to the sixteenth-century reformers.[25] This work brought Ussher to the attention of King James VI, which led to his royal appointment to the See of Meath in 1621, just one day after the death of the previous bishop, George Montgomery. Ussher's new post included a seat on the Irish privy council, giving him cause to spend months at a time in England. This political positioning placed him in an area of significant influence within both the English and Irish church, wherein he worked to defend the interests of Irish protestants, as well as formulate policies against the Roman Catholic majority.[26]

Just four years later, in 1625, Ussher was promoted to the archbishopric of Armagh, following the death of Archbishop Christopher Hampton. It was during his time as archbishop that Ussher had his particular dealings with Robert Blair, the boisterous Scottish Presbyterian who had been

---

[22] Elrington, 'Life of James Ussher', *WJU*, 1:44–47.
[23] Knox, *James Ussher*, 23. Ford, *James Ussher*, 89.
[24] Schaff, *The Creeds of Christendom*, 526; Fesko, *The Theology of the Westminster Standards*, 60.
[25] Ussher, 'De Christianorum Ecclesiarum Successione et Statu historica Explicatio,' *WJU*, 2:1–415.
[26] Ford, *James Ussher*, 118.

brought across the Irish Sea to serve in the Church of Ireland.[27] In his autobiography, Blair recounts that on one occasion he preached before Ussher, 'specially insist[ing] to show that Christ our Lord had instituted no lord bishops in his Kirk, but presbyters and ministers.'[28] Following this sermon, Blair recounts a meeting with Ussher, where the archbishop assured him, 'They think ... to cause me to stretch out my hand against you; but all the world shall never move me to do so.'[29]

Blair's account of this meeting has been interpreted in a variety of ways. The high churchman Elrington disbelieves Blair's account entirely, condemning it as absurd and 'notoriously false.'[30] The Presbyterian historian A F S Pearson finds in Blair's account the seeds of Ussher's supposed 'prescopalianism'.[31] The Irish historian John McCafferty argues that 'instead of Ussher tenderly winking at Blair it seems a good deal more plausible to see him marking his cards and espousing a minimal conformity.'[32] Knox and Ford provide a similar account, seeing an evangelical pragmatism in the archbishop's words.[33] Ford, in particular, compares Ussher's sentiments with that of Robert Elchin, a Scottish bishop serving in the dioceses of Down and Connor, who wrote that Scottish Presbyterians were pastorally effective, popular, inexpensive and available during a time of clerical shortage.[34] Given that Ireland remained a Roman Catholic-dominated country, it seems likely that Ussher's dealings with Blair reflect a principled pragmatism in the young archbishop. He expressed as much in a letter to Christopher Sibthorp, stating that he was content to have clergy who differed 'on matters of inferior note, much less of ceremonies and such other things as appertain to discipline rather than to the doctrine of the Church.'[35] In other words, by Ussher's own admission, the evangelistic and pastoral needs of the

[27] Thomas McCrie and William Row, eds., *The Life of Mr Robert Blair* (Edinburgh: Woodrow Society, 1848), 77–80, 89–91.
[28] McCrie and Row, *The Life of Mr Robert Blair*, 78.
[29] McCrie and Row, *The Life of Mr Robert Blair*, 80.
[30] Elrington, 'Life of James Ussher,' *WJU*, 1:146–50.
[31] Pearson, 'Puritan and Presbyterian Settlements in Ireland 1560–1660' in *Presbyterian Origins*, 5–8.
[32] John McCafferty, 'When Reformations Collide' in A. I. Macinnes and Jane Ohlmeyer, eds., *The Stuart Kingdoms in the Seventeenth Century*, (Dublin: Four Courts, 2002), 200–01.
[33] Knox, *James Ussher*, 180–81.
[34] Ford, *James Ussher*, 166–67.
[35] Ussher, 'The Epistle to Sir Christopher Sibthorp', *WJU*, 4:239.

Irish church outweighed ecclesiastical differences raised by their Scottish neighbours.

Conclusion

The geographical and cultural proximity of Irish and Scottish protestants is a significant factor in the consideration of Irish ecclesiology and ecclesiastical convictions. Although Pearson applies his 'prescopalian' label to the Irish church under James Ussher, it is important to remember that the plantation of Scottish Presbyterians into the Church of Ireland began in 1600, 25 years before Ussher was consecrated archbishop of Armagh.[36] It is beyond doubt that the presence of Presbyterian ministers in the Church of Ireland would have blurred the lines between the two forms of church government in the early seventeenth century. However, the co-mingled ecclesiastical structures inherited by Ussher do not indicate blurred ecclesiological or ecclesiastical convictions held by Ussher. Significant care must be taken, then, when using the presence of Presbyterians in the Church of Ireland as evidence of Ussher's so-called prescopalianism. The nineteenth-century Presbyterian historian James Reid may be correct in arguing that, from a Presbyterian perspective, Ussher's Church of Ireland was 'the most moderate and tolerant Episcopal organisation known to history.'[37] Thus, it is one thing to acknowledge the tolerance of the Church of Ireland towards Presbyterians in the seventeenth century; it is quite another to move from that observation to arguing that Ussher's later work, *The Reduction,* 'professed to unite Prelacy and Presbytery.'[38] As we shall see in the following chapters, Ussher professed to do no such thing.

---

[36] A. T. Q. Stewart, *The Narrow Ground: The Roots of Conflict in Ulster* (London: Faber & Faber, 1989), 38.
[37] James S. Reid, *History of the Presbyterian Church in Ireland,* (New York: R. Carter & Brothers, 1860), 10.
[38] Reid, *History of the Presbyterian Church in Ireland,* 129.

CHAPTER 2

CHIEF PRIESTS: OLD TESTAMENT BISHOPS

This chapter is concerned with Ussher's use of the Old Testament in his defence of episcopal oversight. After briefly outlining the historical context of *The Original of Bishops and Metropolitans*, it will then examine the first three aspects of Ussher's argument: the continuity of office between the Old and New Testament, the continuity of order between the Old and New Testament, and the continuity of activity between the Old and New Testament. In each instance, it will demonstrate that his exegesis stood in line with the writings of both the sixteenth-century reformers, and the early church fathers with which he was so familiar. Finally, it will analyse Ussher's subtle critique of the 'root and branch petition', wherein he highlights both the faulty assumptions of the document and its lack of mature biblical exposition.

The defence of episcopacy 1580–1642

Before considering the first half of Ussher's 'biblical' defence of episcopacy, it is necessary to chart the debate preceding *The Original*. Twenty years before Ussher was born, tensions were rising within the Church of England around the 1559 Prayer Book, particularly with regard to its prescription concerning liturgies and vestments. These tensions were especially felt by those still wholly 'committed to the idea of a comprehensive National Church.'[39] The appointment and policies of John Whitgift increased these tensions as he, and men like Richard Bancroft, produced robust defences of the Church of England's ecclesiastical structure in response to the growing opposition to episcopacy. These ecclesiastical defences went beyond the position of the *Thirty-Nine Articles*, which held that episcopacy was an extension of the crown's rule over 'all estates and degrees committed to their charge by God, whether they be ecclesiastical or temporal' (Article XXXVII).

These new defences presented episcopacy as biblically and historically valid modes of church government. One such defence was John Bridge's

---

[39] W. D. James Cargill Thompson, 'Sir Francis Knollys's Campaign Against the *"Jure Divino"* Theory of Episcopacy,' in C. W. Dugmor, ed., *Studies in the Reformation: Luther to Hooker* (London: Athlone Press, 1980), 95.

A Defence of the Government of the Church of Englande in Ecclesiastical matters.[40] Bridge's *Defence* prompted the publishing of the pseudonymous 'Martin Marprelate' tracts, which called for a radical replacement of episcopacy with a Presbyterian government similar to the continental reformers. As tensions continued to rise, Richard Bancroft preached his famed Paul's Cross sermon in February 1589. Ebenezer Davies has elucidated that, despite first appearances, Bancroft's position that episcopacy had 'divine approbation' due to its apostolic origins is one step removed from a *jure divino*[41] (by divine right) position.[42] In light of Davies' conclusion, James Cargill Thompson argues that Hadrian Saravia's subsequent *De Diversis Ministrorum Evangelii Gradibus* (1590) was the first publication to make a definitive *jure divino* argument for episcopacy.[43] Nevertheless, Bancroft's sermon represents an important stage in the development of the Church of England's doctrine of episcopacy for two reasons. First, unlike Whitgift's writings against Cartwright, or John Bridge's *Defence*, it did not refer to church government as a 'thing indifferent.'[44] Secondly, although arguing for the 'divine approbation' of episcopacy, it did so *without reference* to the authority of the crown.[45] As such, Bancroft's sermon, followed by Saravia's tract, demonstrates that conformist and episcopal apologists 'were gaining new self-confidence' in their defence of episcopacy.[46]

It was into this conflict that Richard Hooker's *Laws of Ecclesiastical Polity* were written. Like Bancroft, Hooker 'chose not to echo fellow-conformist English polemicists who in the 1590s were beginning to emphasise divine

---

[40] John Bridges, *A Defence of the Government established in the Church of Englande for Ecclesiasticall Matters* (London: John Windet, 1587).
[41] Jure divino is the idea that church government is by divine right - in other words that the Bible gives explicit rules for the organisation of church government.
[42] Ebenezer Thomas Davies, *Episcopacy and the Royal Supremacy in the Church of England in the XVIth Century* (Oxford: Blackwell, 1950), 28.
[43] W. D. James Cargill Thompson, 'A Reconsideration of Richard Bancroft's Paul's Cross Sermon of 9 February 1588/9,' *Journal of Ecclesiastical History* 20, no. 2 (1969): 265–66.
[44] John Whitgift, *Works of John Whitgift*, ed. J. Ayre, 3 vols. (Cambridge: Parker Society, 1852), vol. 2, 103, 229–30; Bridges, *A Defence of the Government established in the Church of Englande*, 279.
[45] Cargill Thompson, 'A Reconsideration of Richard Bancroft's Paul's Cross Sermon,' 266.
[46] William P. Haugaard, 'The Preface,' in Speed Hill et al, *LEP*, 6:25–26.

right claims for episcopacy.'[47] Books I to V were published in 1593, whereas Books VI to VIII were posthumously published 55 years later, probably by Ussher himself.[48] Book III argues at length concerning '[w]hether it be necessarie that some particular forme of Church-polity be set downe in scripture', concluding that 'Christ did not meane to set downe particular positive lawes for all thinges in such sorte as Moses did.'[49] Book VII, on the other hand, concludes its fifth chapter by stating, 'let us not fear to be herein bold and peremptory, ... surely the first institution of Bishops was from Heaven, was even of God, the Holy Ghost was the Author of it.'[50]

This apparent contradiction, the unfinished nature of Book VIII – and their delayed publication – has left Books VI to VIII enjoying less prominence than Books I to V in the study of Hooker's ecclesiastical convictions. However, Sommerville demonstrates that Hooker, like most conformists of his time, believed that episcopacy was 'scriptural, apostolic and divine in origin, but it was not therefore immutable or necessary to the Church.'[51] Far from a strict *jure divino* principle, Hooker's position could even be described as moderate, applying a 'subtle distinction between scriptural recommendation of a form of church government and its immutable prescription.'[52] Haugaard summarises that Hooker, along with Whitgift and Bancroft, 'claimed little more than what the Preface to the Prayer Book Ordinal declared: "that from the Apostles tyme, there hath bene these orders of Ministers in Christes church, Bisshopes, Priestes, and Deacons."'[53] It is fitting therefore, to describe Hooker's position as *ius divinium*. However, unlike later *jure divino* positions,

---

[47] Diarmaid MacCulloch, 'Richard Hooker: Invention and Reinvention', *Ecclesiastical Law Journal*, 21 (2019), 139.

[48] Lee W. Gibbs, 'Book VI Introduction,' *LEP*, 6:249.

[49] Richard Hooker, 'The Third Booke,' *LEP*, 1:207, 248.

[50] Hooker, 'The Seventh Booke,' *LEP*, 3:170.

[51] M. R. Sommerville, 'Richard Hooker and his Contemporaries on Episcopacy: an Elizabethan Consensus," *Journal of Ecclesiastical History*, 35, no. 2 (1984): 177–87. Corneliu C. Simut, "Orders of Ministry" in Torrence Kirby, ed., *A Companion to Richard Hooker* (Leiden: Brill, 2008), 412.

[52] Sommerville, 'Richard Hooker,' 187.

[53] Haugaard, 'Preface,' *LEP*, 6:26.

Hooker did not deny the status of 'true church' to those who held to a different form of church government.[54]

The Original of Bishops and Metropolitans

On 11 December 1640, the 'root and branch petition' was presented to the Long Parliament, which opposed 'the government of archbishops and lord bishops, deans and archdeacons', insisting that 'said government, with all its dependencies, roots and branches may be abolished' and government established instead 'according to God's word'.[55] This 'root and branch petition' sparked a pamphlet war in 1641, into which Ussher published the collected work *Certain Briefe Treatises Written by Diverse Learned Men, Concerning the Ancient and Moderne Government of the Church,* within which appeared the first version of 'The Originall of Bishops and Metropolitans.'[56] That same year, he also published *The Iudgement of Doctor Rainholdes Touching the Originall of Episcopacy.*[57] Three years later, Thomas Manton compiled his *Confessions and Proofes of Protestant Divines of Reformed Churches, that Episcopacy is in respect of the Office according to the Word of God, and in respect of the Use the Best,* which contained an expanded version of the first 'Originall', incorporating the material from Ussher's *Iudgement of Doctor Rainholdes.*[58] This booklet works from the later edition of 'The Original' as found in Snoddy's recent volume, as it presents a fuller expression of Ussher's thought than the earlier 1641 edition.[59]

Given the common pursuit of a 'biblical' form of church government by both sides of the debate, it is unsurprising that Ussher opened his *Original* by stating,

---

[54] Patrick Collinson, *The Elizabethan Puritan Movement* (London: Jonathan Cape, 1967), 105.

[55] Samuel R. Gardiner, *Constitutional Documents of the Puritan Revolution, 1625–1660,* 3rd ed. (Oxford: Clarendon Press, 1906), 137–38. Cited in Snoddy, 'General Introduction,' *James Ussher and a Reformed Episcopal Church,* xxviii.

[56] James Ussher, *Certain Briefe Treatises Written by Diverse Learned Men, Concerning the Ancient and Moderne Government of the Church,* (Oxford:, n.p., 1641).

[57] Ussher, 'The Iudgements of Doctor Rainholdes,' *WJU,* 7:75–85.

[58] See Snoddy, *James Ussher and a Reformed Episcopal Church,* 118, n.1.

[59] Ussher, 'The Original of Bishops and Metropolitans,' *WJU,* 7:43–71. Elrington's 17-volume edition of Ussher's *Works* only contains only the 1641 edition, immediately followed by *The Judgment of Doctor Rainoldes.*

The ground of episcopacy is derived partly from the pattern prescribed by God in the Old Testament, and partly from the imitation thereof brought in by the apostles, and confirmed by Christ himself in the time of the New. The government of the Church of the Old Testament was committed to the priests and Levites, unto whom the ministers of the New do now succeed; in like sort as our Lord's Day hath done unto their Sabbath, that it might be fulfilled which was spoken by the prophet, touching the vocation of the Gentiles, 'I will take of them for priests, and for Levites, saith the Lord.'[60]

Although Ussher states that episcopal oversight is only 'derived partly' from the Old Testament, the apostolic and New Testament derivations he offers are built upon the foundations of the pattern presented in the Old Testament. In other words, the government of the church in the New Testament is a succession of the government of the priests and Levites of the Old Testament. Given his role in publishing Hooker's final *Laws* four years later, it should come as no surprise that Ussher's argument echoes Hooker in two distinct ways. First, he argues positively that New Testament ministry follows the 'exemplar of the ministry of the Old Testament.'[61] Secondly, like Hooker and Bancroft, and notably dissimilar to sixteenth-century episcopal apologists, he makes no appeal to the divine right claims for episcopal authority.[62]

Old and New Testament continuity of office

Ussher's first Scripture quotation comes from Isaiah 66:21: 'And some of them also I will take for priests and for Levites, says the LORD.' In its original context, Isaiah 66:21 is the climactic end of Isaiah's vision: the eschatological restoration of the people of Israel, with whom the Gentiles will be joined as brothers (Isa 66:20), some of whom will even become priests and Levites. Gentile ordination is intimated earlier in Isaiah's vision, where he promises that 'foreigners who join' will be allowed to minister to God, serve him and make burnt offerings and sacrifices (Isa

---

[60] Ussher, *OB*, 118.
[61] Corneliu C. Simut, 'Orders of Ministry' in Kirby, *A Companion to Richard Hooker*, 412. Hooker, *LEP*, 5:78.
[62] McCulloch, 'Richard Hooker: Invention and Reinvention,' 139.

56:6–7). Isaiah 66:21, however, is the only place in the Old Testament that speaks explicitly of Gentiles being made priests and Levites. Given its prophetic genre and its eschatological tone, it is not immediately clear whether Isaiah 66 is concerned specifically with the nature of Gentile new covenant ministry, or whether it is merely an illustration of the egalitarian nature of the new covenant.

This egalitarian reading was first popularised at the earliest stages of the Reformation. On the 22 February 1530, Martin Luther concluded his three-year lecture series on Isaiah by stating that Isaiah 66:21 stood as a declaration that 'the priesthood has been shifted from a single tribe of the Jews to all nations. We are all priests.'[63] Although Luther appears to have never used the phrase 'priesthood of all believers', the concept was a central doctrine for the German reformations.[64] Despite its centrality for those reformations, John McNeill notes likewise that 'Calvin's utterances specifically on the priesthood of believers are rare and unsystematic, although in treatment of other topics he gives to that doctrine substantially the content given to it by Luther.'[65] One place where Calvin does address the doctrine, yet differs from Luther, is in his commentary on Isaiah 66:21. There he states that although some

> expound this doctrine in a general matter... [Isaiah] appears to describe in an especial manner ministers and teachers whom the Lord also chose from among the Gentiles, and appointed to execute this distinguished office; that is, to preach the Gospel; such as Luke, Timothy, and others of the same class, who offered spiritual sacrifices to God by the Gospel.[66]

Ussher, then, like Calvin before him, understood these verses to communicate the continuation of ministerial offices under the new

---

[63] Martin Luther, 'Lectures on Isaiah Chapters 40–66' in *The Works of Martin Luther,* Herbert J. A. Bouman et al., trans; J. Pelikan and H. Lehmann, eds., 55 vols. (Saint Louis, MS: Concordia, 1958–1986), vol. 17, 415.
[64] Timothy J. Wengert, *Priesthood, Pastors, Bishops: Public Ministry for the Reformation and Today* (Minneapolis, MN: Fortress Press, 2008), 1.
[65] John T. McNeill in John Calvin, *Institutes of the Christian Religion,* vol. 1; ed. John T. McNeill; trans. Ford Lewis Battles (Louisville: Westminster John Knox Press, 1960), 502 n.15.
[66] John Calvin, *Commentary on the Book of the Prophet Isaiah,* trans. William Pringle, 4 vols. (Grand Rapids: Eerdmans, 1956), vol. 4, 437.

covenant. Given both Ussher and Calvin's reading of Isaiah 66:21, and Ussher's influence on the Westminster Assembly, it is not surprising that these verses are also employed in a similar manner in the *Westminster Standards*.[67]

Ussher's particularist reading of Isaiah 66:21 can also be found throughout the church fathers. In the first century, Clement of Rome identified the same analogy between priests and Levites, bishops and deacons in his Corinthian epistle.[68] In the third century, Cyprian aligns Levitical service and presbyterial ministry.[69] In the fourth century, Peter, Bishop of Alexandria, identifies Arius' diaconate, as opposed to priesthood, as being 'only endowed with the dignity of a Levite.'[70] Again, in the fifth century, Jerome understood Isaiah 66:21 as the grounds of the Apostle Paul's words in 1 Corinthians 4:1, 'This is how one should regard us, as servants of Christ and stewards of the mysteries of God.'[71]

Unlike the early church fathers, it is not entirely clear whether for Ussher the priests and Levites were analogous to bishops and presbyters, bishops and deacons, or presbyters and deacons. What is clear, however, is that Ussher's derivation from Old Testament ministry to New Testament ministry, based on Isaiah 66:21, finds its roots in the patristic and reformed tradition with which he was so familiar.

Old and New Testament continuity of order

Having established this derivation between Old and New Testament ministry, Ussher proceeds to give a detailed breakdown of the orders of the Old Testament ministry.[72] He argues that just as there was distinction *between* the priests and the Levites, so too was there a distinction *within* the priests and the Levites. The Levites were divided into three families, each with their own נשיא, אי pri or ruler (Num 3:24, 30, 35). Similarly, the priests were set into 24 divisions, with each division having their own head (1 Chron 24:1–4). This order continued throughout the Old

---

[67] *WCF*, 590–92.
[68] Clement, 'First Epistle to the Corinthians,' *ANF*, 1:16.
[69] Cyprian, 'Epistle LI', *ANF*, 5:322.
[70] Peter of Alexandria, 'The Genuine Acts of Peter,' *ANF*, 6:263.
[71] Jerome, 'Commentary on Isaiah 18.31–32,' *PG*, 70:1445–48. Mark W. Elliot, trans., *Ancient Christian Commentary on Scripture: Old Testament XI: Isaiah 40–66*, (Downers Grove: IVP, 2007), 289.
[72] Ussher, *OB*, 118.

Testament period, the inter-testamental period, and into the Gospels themselves, as evidenced by the presence of 'chief priests' (ἐ ief pri) in the gospels (Matt 2:4; Mark 2:26; Luke 3:2).

After demonstrating the different orders of ministry in the Old Testament, Ussher highlights the hierarchy within those orders. He does this by drawing attention to both the LXX and Vulgate translations of פקד in Numbers 11. Both the Levites and the priests are spoken of as having פקד over them, which the LXX translates ἐover the (Neh 11:22), and the Vulgate translates *episcopus* (Neh 11:22, cf 11:9, 14). Pre-empting any opposition to the validity of the LXX's translation, Ussher highlights that פקד is rendered as ἐis rende in the New Testament by the Apostle Peter, when he translates פקד in Psalm 109:9 as ἐPsalm 10 in Acts 1:20. Again, just as Ussher did not draw a neat parallel between Old Testament priests and Levites, and New Testament presbyters and deacons, neither does he draw neat parallels between Old and New Testament ἐn Acts 1.[73] Ussher's argument, rather, is simply that there was both a twofold order of Old Testament ministry, and that overseers were appointed over those orders, as demonstrated by the use of the term ἐold orde throughout the LXX.

Old and New Testament continuity of activity

After establishing the hierarchies of Old Testament ministry, Ussher argues for the continuity of activity between Old and New Testament ministry. Quoting Moses' final words to the twelve tribes of Israel, Ussher shows that these Old Testament ministers had two distinct jobs: to teach and to sacrifice (Deut 33:10). The sacrificial aspect of Old Testament ministry had 'ceased ... the truth prefigured thereby being now exhibited [in Christ].'[74] However, the absence of a typological fulfilment of the teaching aspect of Old Testament ministry, alongside the New Testament's emphasis on teaching, suggests that New Testament teachers continue to perform this work in a similar way.[75] Just as priests and Levites had the responsibility of teaching God's people, so too bishops and presbyters must be 'διδακτικοί, "apt to teach", able by sound doctrine

---

[73] One could imagine, for example, that if priests and Levites were analogous to bishops and deacons, that a further analogy could be drawn between chief priests and archbishops, and ruling Levites and archdeacons.

[74] Ussher, *OB,* 119.

[75] Ussher, *OB,* 119.

both to exhort and to convince the gainsayers.'[76] Thus, the New Testament activity of ministerial teaching was a continuation of the Old Testament activity of ministerial teaching.

Old and New Testament continuity proved

A similar argument concerning the continuity of teaching can be found in Ambrose's *Three Books on the Duties of the Clergy*.[77] Likewise, the later *Westminster Standards* considered the new covenant's teaching ministry as a continuation of that aspect of the old covenant's teaching ministry.[78] However, rather than turn to Ambrose for support, the archbishop seeks to prove this continuity from the Apostle Paul. Ussher wrote that:

> God had appointed, that 'the priests, the Levites, and all the tribe of Levi should eat the offerings of the Lord made by fire', doth not the apostle by just analogy infer from thence, that forasmuch as 'they which waited on the altar, were partakers with the altar; even so had the Lord ordained, that they which preach the Gospel, should live on the Gospel?'[79]

As we have seen from his treatment of the word ἐς we hav and the activity of teaching, Ussher is neither arguing for a simplistic correlation of vocabulary, nor a complete replacement of Old Testament priests with New Testament presbyters. Rather, he is attempting to read the Old Testament the same way that the Apostle Paul read the Old Testament. Just as Paul drew a line between the support of the Old and New Testament ministers, so too Ussher drew a line between the activity of Old and New Testament ministers. Just as Old Testament priests and Levites were sustained by their ministry at the altar, so too New Testament pastors are sustained by their ministry of proclaiming the gospel.

---

[76] Ussher, *OB*, 119. Biblical quotations from 1 Timothy 3:2, and Titus 1:9, respectively.

[77] Ambrose, 'Book I,' *NPNF* 2/10:41.

[78] *WCF*, 590.

[79] Ussher, *OB*, 119–20. Citing 1 Cor 9:13–14.

The breaking of biblical continuity

If then, according to Ussher, the Old Testament promised Gentile priests and Levites, and the apostle drew an analogy between priests and preachers, Ussher asks:

> With what shew of reason then can any man imagine, that what was instituted by God in the Law, for mere matter of government and preservation of good order, (without all respect of type or ceremony,) should now be rejected in the Gospel, as a device of Antichrist? that what was by the Lord once 'planted a noble vine, wholly a right seed', should now be so 'turned into the degenerate plant of a strange vine;' that no purging or pruning of it will serve the turn, but it must be cut down root and branch, as 'a plant which our heavenly Father had never planted?'[80]

In other words, if God established a good order in the Old Testament, how can an analogous order now be condemned as a device of the Antichrist? The ceasing of the 'type and ceremony' of the sacrificial system should not necessitate the cessation of all Old Testament structures. Ussher's use of the phrase 'cut down root and branch' indicates that the signatories of the 'root and branch petition' are in his sights. Given the root and branch imagery, Ussher's horticultural Bible quotations in this section appear to be mere variations on a theme. However, a closer look at the broader context of both chapters suggest a deeper critique of the 'root and branch' signatories is taking place.

The biblical text, Jeremiah 2:21, quoted by Ussher, speaks of Israel's status as God's people despite the failings of their clergy, and despite the fact that 'those who handle the law did not know me' (Jer 2:8). Similarly, the quotation from Matthew 15:13 concerns Israel's first-century teachers, the Pharisees. Both Matthew 15 and Jeremiah 2, therefore, address the issue of the faithless leaders of God's people. The 'root and branch petition' opens by stating that its primary desire was that 'said government with all its dependencies, roots and branches, may be abolished, and all laws in their behalf made void, and the government

---

[80] Ussher, *OB*, 120. Biblical quotations from Jeremiah 2:21 and Matthew 15:13, respectively.

according to God's word may be rightly placed amongst us.'[81] Despite its stated desire for a church government formed 'according to God's word', the substance of the document only addresses 'the manifold evils, pressures, and grievances caused, practised and occasioned by the prelates and their dependents.'[82] The petition never addresses the lack of biblical evidence for the episcopal office. Ussher's use of Matthew and Jeremiah, therefore, address the actual issues the 'root and branch petition' raised – ungodly leaders – rather than the issue it professed to address: an ecclesiastical system 'according to God's word'. Thus, just as the presence of ungodly priests and Levites in the Old Testament did not negate the office of priest and Levite, so too the presence of ungodly prelates does not negate the office of bishop.

Conclusion

The question concerning a biblical model of church government dominated the seventeenth-century Church of England. Unlike his Presbyterian opponents or episcopalian predecessors, Ussher built a cumulative case (as opposed to a strict *jure divino* case) for the Old Testament origins of episcopal oversight. From the Old Testament, he outlined a threefold model that continued into the first century, as evidenced in the gospels: chief priests, priests and Levites. In several places, these chief priests were also given the title ἐLevites.. The Old Testament indicated a continuity of ministry into the new covenant: priests and Levites will be drawn, not just from the tribe of Levi, but from Gentiles grafted into the people of God. This promise, alongside the New Testament's appeal to such a continuity, indicates that there is a significant, though not absolute, continuity between Old and New Testament ministries. Having established the first part of his argument – that his ecclesiastical structure is partly derived from the Old Testament – Ussher needed to demonstrate that this model is imitated by the apostles and confirmed in the New Testament.[83] It is to that confirmation we will now turn.

---

[81] 'Root and Branch Petition' in Henry Gee and William John Hardy, eds., *Documents Illustrative of English Church History* (New York: Macmillan, 1896), 538.

[82] 'Root and Branch Petition,' 538.

[83] Ussher, *OB*, 118.

CHAPTER 3

ANGELS: NEW TESTAMENT BISHOPS

While the previous chapter presented Ussher's Old Testament defence of episcopacy, this chapter will consider Ussher's statement that episcopacy was 'confirmed by Christ himself in the time of the New.'[84] Ussher's New Testament defence is markedly different from his Old Testament defence, in both scope and method. Whereas his Old Testament defence covered a wide gamut of biblical history, drawing upon 11 books of the Bible and 17 different chapters, his New Testament defence contains detailed exposition of a handful of verses from the first three chapters of Revelation.[85] Alongside a narrower scope of Biblical data, this section contains the archbishop's most sustained use of secondary sources across *The Original* and *The Reduction*. The detailed exposition and secondary source engagement suggests that this was the most contested aspect of Ussher's defence. The sources – Thomas Brightman and Theodore Beza, neither of whom were episcopalians – would have particularly appealed to Ussher's Presbyterian readers. Although the archbishop agrees with Brightman's and Beza's exegetical decisions, he disagrees with their ecclesiastical conclusions, seeing them as inconsistent with their own exegesis. In doing so, he appeals to his readers to do the same.

The words and hand of Christ

Ussher's New Testament defence begins with the opening chapters of the book of Revelation. These three chapters are presented as the very words of Jesus, dictated to the Apostle John, for the seven churches across Asia Minor. Their dictated status is important for the archbishop, as he understands them to present an opportunity to 'consult with Christ himself.'[86] He begins his exposition by citing the letter to the church in Sardis (Rev 3:1–6). This letter opens by stating that the seven stars –

---

[84] Ussher, *OB*, 118.
[85] The 17 Old Testament chapters considered are Numbers 3; Deuteronomy 33; 18; 1 Chronicles 24; Ezra 8; Nehemiah 11; Psalms 109; Isaiah 66; Jeremiah 2; Matthew 2; 15; 27; 1 Corinthians 9; Hebrews 4.
[86] Ussher, *OB*, 120.

previously identified as the angels of the seven churches (Rev 1:16, 20) – are owned by Christ. After the Scripture quotation, Ussher immediately restates that Christ 'owneth then, we see, these stars.'[87] This repeated stress on the ownership of Christ reemphasises the divine (as opposed to human) origin of church offices and their authority. These stars, 'which thou sawest in my right hand, are the angels of the seven churches', derive their authority and office from Christ himself.[88]

Thomas Brightman

Ussher then commends and cites the clergyman and commentator, Thomas Brightman (1562–1607). Brightman was a Church of England clergyman from Nottingham known for his Presbyterian sympathies and his posthumously published commentary on Revelation.[89] Ussher begins by commending Brightman as 'a learned man, very much devoted to the now so highly admired discipline' of exegesis.[90] Citing Brightman, Ussher writes 'how great is the dignity of true pastors, who are both STARS, fixed in no other firmament than in the right hand of Christ, and ANGELS?'[91] Throughout the LXX and the New Testament, ἄγγελος repeatedly refers to human messengers. The archbishop was no stranger to intertextual vocabulary arguments, having previously argued from four verses of the LXX and New Testament's usage of ἐπισκοπή. However, in this instance, rather than appeal to the abundance of lexical data on ἄγγελος, he appeals to a Presbyterian pastor to defend his position. In order to understand why Brightman was employed, it is necessary to briefly examine his Revelation commentary, which was enjoying particular prominence in Ussher's day.

Brightman's commentary was a significant publication for reformed English eschatology. Alongside Joseph Mede's *Key of the Revelation Searched and Demonstrated,* Brightman's *Revelation* was central for the advancement of the literalist, historical interpretation of the book of

---

[87] Ussher, *OB,* 120. Cited from Rev 3:1.
[88] Ussher, *OB,* 120. Cited from Rev 1:20.
[89] Thomas Brightman, *A Revelation of the Apocalyps* (Amsterdam: Thomas Stafford, 1611).
[90] Ussher, *OB,* 120.
[91] Ussher, *OB,* 120. Capitalisation original. Cited from Brightman, *A Revelation of the Apocalyps,* 31.

Revelation.[92] For example, according to Brightman, the Laodicean church was the Church of England, a commingling of 'prudent and moderate men in the matter of Religion, such as we call at this day *Statists, or moderate and direct Protestants of State,* and which are commonly known to be *lukewarm professours* ... the mixture whereof this *mungrell lukewarmnesse* had his being and beginning.'[93] Just as Christ promised to spit the Laodiceans out of his mouth (Rev 3:16), so too would he 'speweth ... the English Angels, unless they prevent it by repentance.'[94] In contrast with the lukewarm Church of England, the Church of Scotland was the faithful, enduring Philadelphian church.[95] Given these exegetical conclusions, Ussher's initial use and commendation of Brightman would have won him no favours from the conformist wing in the English church.

Although Brightman's historicism marked a turning point in the interpretation of Revelation in the English reformed church, his identification of the angels as ministers finds its roots in Augustine, who argued that what is contained in the seven letters to the churches 'could not be said to the heavenly angels, who retain their love unchanged', and therefore must refer to the ministers of those churches.[96] Bullinger, likewise, identifies angels as 'pastours of churches', symbolised as angels to signify the 'faith and diligence of ministers', confirmed by their location alongside the tribes of Israel and the apostles on the twelve gates of the new Jerusalem (Rev 21:12–14).[97] Brightman's interpretative methods therefore, while in many ways 'pioneer[ing] in the field of apocalyptic interpretation', on the identity of the angels borrowed significantly from the Augustinian heritage with which Ussher would have been so familiar.[98] It is almost certain, then, that Ussher's positive use of Brightman was significantly strategic. Rather than appeal to the Augustinian tradition respected by conformists and nonconformists

[92] William M. Lamont, *Richard Baxter and the Millennium* (London: Croom Helm, 1979), 14.
[93] Brightman, *A Revelation of the Apocalyps,* 44. Italics original.
[94] Brightman, *A Revelation of the Apocalyps,* 44.
[95] Brightman, *A Revelation of the Apocalyps,* 42.
[96] Augustine, 'Letter XLIII,' *NPNF* 1/1:283.
[97] Heinrich Bullinger, *A Hundred Sermons vpo the Apocalips of Jesu Christe,* trans. John Daus (London: Iohn Daus, 1561), 45, 651, 240.
[98] Lamont, *Godly Rule,* 50.

alike, he uses an argument made by a Presbyterian Puritan regarding the pastoral identity of the angels in Revelation 2–3.

Ephesian plurality and synonymity

Having lauded Brightman as 'a learned man', Ussher then asserts that Brightman must have 'considered well that in the church of Ephesus, one of the seven here pointed at, there were many PRESBYTERS.'[99] By stating that Brightman must have considered the Ephesian church, Ussher is appealing to his readers to consider the same. Luke's account of its establishment is his longest treatment of one church in Acts (Acts 19–20), perhaps because it was so large, or perhaps because it is where the Apostle Paul spent three years of his ministry. Its size is emphasised in Acts 19, where the number of converts threatens the city's idol economy, causing the whole city to riot (Acts 19:23–41). Given the size of the Ephesian church and the plurality of presbyters over its congregations (Acts 20:17), Ussher demonstrates that if Brightman's exegesis is correct, 'by admitting one angel there above the rest ... he should be forced also to acknowledge the eminency of one bishop above the other bishops (the name being in those days common unto all the presbyters).'[100]

That Ussher should draw attention to the synonymity of πρεσβUssher and ὲand Ussh in Paul's farewell discourse may at first glance appear to weaken his argument of the primacy of bishops. The synonymity of the terms was central to the Presbyterian argument against episcopal oversight.[101] Indeed, in his introduction to Ussher's *Original*, Snoddy comments that in this instance, Ussher 'conceded that there was a plurality of elders in the church of Ephesus, and the name "elder" was then interchangeable with "bishop".'[102] However, Ussher's acknowledgement of the terms' interchangeability in this passage is not necessarily a concession to the Presbyterians, because the synonymity of πρεσβver, Usand ὲnd βver, was not in the first instance a Presbyterian argument. Of all the church fathers, Jerome states the argument most clearly in his epistle to Oceanus, where he writes that 'with the ancients

---

99 Ussher, *OB*, 120. Capitalisation original.

100 Ussher, *OB*, 120–21.

101 See John Milton, 'Of Prelatical Episcopacy (1641)' in Douglas Bush et al., eds., *The Complete Prose Works of John Milton*, 6 vols. (New Haven: Yale University Press, 1953–73), vol. 1, 625. Travers, *A Full and Plaine Declaration of Ecclesiastical Discipline*.ou

102 Snoddy, 'General Introduction,' in *James Ussher*, xxxi.

these names were synonymous, one alluding to office, the other to the age of the clergy.'[103] Similarly, at the outset of the English Reformation, Cranmer notes that bishops and presbyters 'were not two things, but both one office in the beginning of Christ's religion.'[104] Therefore, while his Presbyterian opponents made much of the synonymity of presbyter and bishop in the New Testament text, Ussher's parenthetical comment on that synonymity was merely a reflection of Cranmer and Jerome before him.

Having first lauded Brightman and his preliminary exegetical work on Revelation 2:1, Ussher concludes his section by demonstrating the negative impact of Brightman's ecclesiastical convictions on his exegetical conclusions. Two pages after identifying the angel of Ephesus as a pastor, Brightman retracts his earlier words by pluralising the angel of Ephesus as 'not one Angell alone at Ephesus but many, neither yet any Prince amonge these.'[105] In response, the archbishop removes his proverbial gloves, critiquing Brightman's conclusions as the result of a 'poor pretence of a poor show of some shallow reasons.'[106] Ussher continues, stating that this 'wresting of the plain words of our Saviour is so extreme[ly] violent.'[107] In other words, according to Ussher, Brightman saw the inconsistency of his exegesis with Presbyterianism, and rather than concede any form of primacy in the early church, pluralises that which Christ had expressed as singular.[108]

Theodore Beza

After his judicious usage of Thomas Brightman, Ussher appealed to a second authority on New Testament exegesis: Calvin's successor in the Republic of Geneva, Theodore Beza. Beza's famous *De vera excommunicatione et Christiano presbyterio* – written against Thomas Erastus' *Explicatio gravissimae quaestionis utrum excommunicatio* – marked him as another unlikely ecclesiastical source for the divine right

---

[103] Jerome, 'Letter XIX. To Oceanus,' *NPNF* 2/6:288.
[104] Thomas Cranmer, 'Questions and Answers Concerning the Sacraments and the Appointment and Power of Bishops and Priests' in John E. Cox, ed., *Miscellaneous Writings and Letters of Thomas Cranmer* (Cambridge: Parker Society, 1846), 117.
[105] Brightman, *A Revelation of the Apocalyps*, 33.
[106] Ussher, *OB*, 121.
[107] Ussher, *OB*, 121.
[108] Ussher, *OB*, 121.

absolutist Ussher.[109] The archbishop himself recognised as much, noting that Beza was 'zealously affected to the advancement of the new discipline [of Presbyterian government].'[110] Indeed, Beza was so opposed to England's ecclesiastical system that, in correspondence with Scottish ministers, he refers to England as a 'minor Babylon.'[111] Despite Beza's zeal for this 'new discipline', he too records in his annotations that these angels ought to be understood as 'the president [προεστes], as whom it behoved specially to be admonished touching those matters; and by him, both the rest of his colleagues, and the whole church likewise.'[112] This identification of a προεστid or presidential figure by Beza will be crucial for the next stage of Ussher's argument, as that same figure will be distinguished by Ignatius as 'the single and constant president thereof, from the rest of the number of presbyters, by appropriating the name of bishop unto him.'[113]

New Testament patterns

Although Ussher will go on to cite Justin Martyr's *Apology* wherein he refers to Timothy as a προεστη , the identification of the angels in Revelation 1–3, cross-referenced with Acts 19–20, are the archbishop's only New Testament evidences for episcopal oversight.[114] Remarkably, no references are made to the pastoral epistles, which were commonplace among publications on episcopal oversight, such as that of Thomas Bilson:

> He is a Bishop, which is first amongst the Presbyters,
> so that every Bishop is a Presbyter, but every Presbyter

---

[109] Theodore Beza, *Tractatus pius et moderatus de vera excommunicatione, et christiano presbyterio* (Geneva: Jean Le Preux, 1590). Thomas Erastus, *Explicatio gravissimæ Quæstionis, utrùm excommunicatio quatenus religionem intelligentes et amplexantes, a Sacramentorum usu, propter admissum facinus arcet, manadato nitatur Divino, an excogitata sit ab hominibus* (London: Pésclavii, 1589). Tadataka Maruyama, *The Ecclesiology of Theodore Beza: The Reform of the True Church* (Geneva: Librairie Droz, 1978), 25–38.

[110] Ussher, *OB*, 121.

[111] William Ferguson, *Scotland's Relations with England: A Survey to 1707* (Edinburgh: Saltire Society, 1994), 90.

[112] Theodore Beza, *Annotationes Maiores in Novum DN. Nostri Iesu Christi Testamentum*, 2 vols. (Geneva, 1594), vol. 2, 635. Cited in Ussher, OB, 121.

[113] Ussher, *OB*, 122.

[114] Ussher, *OB*, 122.

is not a Bishop. (For example) Paul signifieth that he made Timothy a Presbyter, but because he had none other before him, he was a Bishop. Whereupon Paul showeth him how he should ordain a Bishop: for it was neither meet, nor lawful, that the inferiour should ordain the greater, or superiour. No man can give that which he hath not received.[115]

Given Ussher's grounding in the church fathers and the nature of Presbyterian arguments for episcopacy, it is surprising that Ussher spends so little time on New Testament ministry, especially when compared with his previous Old Testament defence and the proceeding arguments from the church fathers. Precisely why he omits the pastoral epistles is difficult to discern. However, when considered in light of his opening statement: 'THE GROUND of episcopacy is derived partly from the pattern prescribed by God in the Old Testament, and partly from the imitation thereof brought in by the apostles, and confirmed by Christ himself in the time of the New', the rationale behind the weighting of Ussher's argument begins to emerge.[116] Ussher's argument, then, is not that episcopacy is explicitly prescribed in the New Testament. Rather, the pattern of the Old Testament is imitated and confirmed in the New Testament. Where other defences of episcopacy focused on the function of the episcopal office, Ussher's defence is merely concerned with the identification of a biblical pattern of leadership, rather than the leader's office or function.

Conclusion

Just as the priests and Levites of the Old Testament had episcopal figures over them, so too the New Testament has episcopal figures overseeing the leaders of the church. These figures are confirmed by Christ in Revelation 1–3, wherein he addresses a presidential figure over each church to encourage and rebuke them. This identification of the angels as presidential figures can even be found in the exegesis of prominent Presbyterians. However, according to Ussher, their ecclesiastical conclusions are out of step with their exegetical insights. Having demonstrated Christ's confirmation of this Old Testament ecclesiastical

---

[115] Thomas Bilson, *The Perpetual Government of Christ's Church* (London: Christopher Barker, 1593), 217–218.
[116] Ussher, *OB*, 118.

structure, Ussher turns his attention to his particular area of expertise: the imitation of this structure by the apostles and fathers of the early church.

CHAPTER 4

THE FATHERS: EARLY CHURCH BISHOPS

Although the opening of *The Original* states that episcopacy is derived from the Scriptures, the comparative weight given to church history suggests that the prescription of ministerial offices in the writings of the early church are especially significant for Ussher's argument. Of the twenty-two pages occupied by the final edition of *The Original* in Morton's *Confessions and Proofes of Protestant Divines of Reformed Churches,* three and half pages are dedicated to the biblical data, with the remaining nineteen given to the presence and nature of bishops and presbyteries from the first century to the council of Nicaea.

Ussher's historical defence of episcopacy outlines numerous episcopal figures spanning the first four centuries of the Christian church. He begins by examining texts both concerning and written by the three chief Apostolic Fathers: Ignatius, Polycarp and Clement. From these three fathers he establishes the 'central, but cooperative' role of bishops and presbyteries in the earliest days of the church.[117] According to Ussher, this survey proves that episcopacy was practised 'from the apostolical times', corroborating his exegetical decision regarding the angels in Revelation 2–3.[118] As such, although the weighting of the material in *The Original* appears imbalanced, for Ussher, the historical data is not separate from his exegesis of the biblical text, but rather supports it.

Ussher's conclusion on the origin of episcopacy is not, however, the conclusion of *The Original.* Having established the origin of bishops, he goes on to argue for not just bishops, but metropolitans.[119] His argument for metropolitans is also based on the seven epistles from Revelation, with each church, due to their regional status in Roman Asia, functioning metropolitically over the other churches in the region. Space precludes a comprehensive analysis of this section of Ussher's argument, thus this chapter will focus on the earlier – and crucial –

---

[117] Ford, *Ussher,* 239.
[118] Ussher, *OB,* 135.
[119] An archbishop, or diocesan bishop over suffragan bishops.

aspect of his historical argument. In other words, this chapter will consider the episcopacy of Timothy and the Apostolic Fathers, to determine whether or not Ussher had in fact deduced episcopacy from the time of the apostles. Narrowing the focus to these earliest writings seems fitting, given the archbishop's own position, borrowed from Tertullian: 'whatever comes first is true, whatever comes after is an adultery.'[120]

Timothy

Recruited by the Apostle Paul on his second missionary journey, Timothy accompanied Paul around modern-day Turkey and Greece, before being left by Paul in Ephesus on his third missionary journey (Acts 16:1; 19:21; 1 Tim 1:3). As the previous chapter noted, Timothy was understood, even by Beza, to be the προεστrk, 'or president of the Ephesian presbytery.'[121] In the early church, προεστ e was used interchangeably with bishop, evidenced by Ussher from Justin Martyr, Dionysius of Corinth, and Marcellus of Ancyra.[122] Ussher then cites five sources that directly refer to Timothy as a bishop. The first reference is the subheading 'the first Bishop of Ephesus' in particular biblical manuscripts of 2 Timothy.[123] The second reference is Eusebius' *Ecclesiastical History* which notes that he was 'the first to receive the episcopate' of Ephesus.[124] The third is Photius who, when writing of Timothy's martyrdom, stated that 'the history declares Timothy to have been the first Bishop of Ephesus ... that the Apostle Timothy was ordained and enthroned bishop of the metropolis of Ephesus by great Paul.'[125] The fourth was Polycrates, himself the eighth bishop of Ephesus.[126] The final reference to Timothy concerns his assistance of the Apostle John upon the latter's move to Ephesus

---

[120] Elrington, 'Life of James Ussher,' *WJU*, 1:9. 'verum quodcunque primum, adulterum quodcunque posterius.'
[121] Ussher, *OB*, 123. Citing Beza, *Annotationes*, vol. 2, 459.
[122] Justin, 'Apologia Prima 67,' *PG*, 6:429. Eusebius, 'Church History,' *NPNF* 2/1:200. Marcellus of Ancrya, *The Panarion of Epiphanius of Salamis, Books II and III*. De Fide. trans. Frank Williams, (Leiden: Brill, 2013), 434.
[123] Ussher, *OB*, 123. Mss. K, L, Textus Receptus. See Bruce Metzger, *A Textual Commentary on the Greek New Testament*, 2nd ed. (Stuttgart: Deutsche Bibelgesellschaft, 1994), 583.
[124] Eusebius, 'Church History,' *NPNF* 2/1:136.
[125] Photius, 'Bibliotheca 254,' *PG*, 20:496B
[126] Polycrates, 'De Martyrio Timothei,' *Historiae Plurimorum Sanctorum* (Louvain, 1485), fols. xvi^r-xvii^r

following his release from Patmos.[127] John is described as taking up government 'with the assistance of SEVEN bishops.'[128] This move to Ephesus by John is then supported by citations from Irenaeus, Eusebius and Jerome.[129]

Given the prominence of Timothy in the New Testament, it is not surprising that Ussher cites so many secondary sources that confirm his thesis. What is surprising, however, is that unlike the following episcopal presentations, Ussher's citations make no mention of nature of Timothy's episcopate, merely its existence. That being said, the repeated reference to Timothy as bishop, as opposed to presbyter, does lend support to the idea that even within the life of the apostles and their immediate successors, the synonymity of bishop and presbyter was beginning to disappear.

Ignatius of Antioch

In 1644, the same year that the longer form of *The Original* was published, Ussher also published his non-interpolated edition of the Ignatian corpus. This critical work was necessary, given the objections of the Puritan John Milton, who had sought to discredit all of Ignatius' writings as untrustworthy due to the interpolation of later writers.[130] Ussher's work silenced Milton's textual objections to Ignatius, and remained an important source for Ignatian scholarship into the nineteenth century.[131] Given the significance of Ignatius for monepiscopal debates,[132] and Ussher's own Ignatian expertise, it is no surprise that he is referenced more than any other early church father in *The Original*.

Ussher begins by stressing that Ignatius wrote 'within no greater compass of time than twelve years' after the writing of Revelation.[133] This

---

[127] Ussher, *OB*, 133.
[128] Ussher, *OB*, 133. Capitalisation original. Citing Photius, 'Bibliotheca 254,' *PG*, 104:103A, 104:A.
[129] Irenaeus, 'Against Heresies,' *ANF* 1:414, 416. Eusebius, 'Church History,' *NPNF* 2/1:150. Jerome, 'Lives of Illustrious Men,' *NPNF* 2/3:364–65; Jerome, 'Preface to Matthew,' *NPNF* 2/6:495.
[130] Don M. Wolfe, 'Introduction' in Bush et al., *Complete Prose Works of John Milton,* vol. 1, 118–121.
[131] J. B. Lightfoot, *The Apostolic Fathers* (London: Macmillan, 1907), 102.
[132] Monarchical episcopacy, as opposed to collegial episcopacy.
[133] Ussher, *OB*, 122.

chronological proximity to the apostles is defended by Ussher through his citation of Irenaeus' *Against Heresies,* Eusebius' *Church History,* and Jerome's *Lives of Illustrious Men.*[134] Ussher then proceeds to demonstrate that Ignatius was more than chronologically proximate to the apostles; he was actually ordained by the apostles. Ussher cites the following: Theodoret, himself a bishop of Antioch; John of Antioch; and Felix, Bishop of Rome; all of whom testify that Ignatius was ordained Bishop of Antioch by the Apostle Peter.[135] John Chrysostom, who had served as a priest in the Antiochean church before being made Bishop of Constantinople, is then cited, declaring that Ignatius 'obtained this office from those saints, and the hands of the blessed apostles touched that sacred head.'[136] For Ussher, the chronological and ministerial proximity of Ignatius to the apostles marks his 'clear testimony' on the presence and nature of episcopacy as second only to the Scriptures themselves.[137]

Having established the provenance of Ignatius, Ussher then draws attention to Ignatius' Ephesian and Smyrnaean epistles. With each reference, Ussher draws attention not only to the presence of a bishop, but also the bishop's unity with the wider presbytery – an important aspect of his subsequently published *The Reduction of Episcopacy.* Firstly, in Ignatius' letter to the Ephesians, Ussher summarises Ignatius' blessing of their bishop, Onesimus, before twice quoting him on the unity of the bishop with the presbytery. Ignatius commended the church because their 'presbytery ... being "so conjoined", as he saith, "with their bishop, as the strings are with the harp"; and toward the end exhorteth them to "obey both the bishop and the presbytery, with an undivided mind."'[138] Similarly, Ussher records Ignatius' words to the Smyrnaean church, 'wherein he also saluteth their bishop and presbytery, exhorting all the people to "follow their bishop, as Christ Jesus did his Father, and the presbytery, as the apostles", and telling them that no man ought either to administer the sacraments, or do any thing appertaining to the church, without the consent of the bishop.'[139]

---

[134] Ussher, *OB,* 124. Irenaeus, 'Against Heresies,' *ANF,* 1:559–60. Eusebius, *PG,* 19:551–52. Jerome, 'Lives of Illustrious Men,' *NPNF 2,* 3:167–68.

[135] Theodoret, 'Eranistes, Dialogus 1,' *PG,* 83:81A. Felix, *PL,* 58:919A.

[136] John Chrysostom, *PG,* 50:588. trans. Snoddy, *James Ussher and a Reformed Episcopal Church,* 124, n.44.

[137] Ussher, *OB,* 122.

[138] Ussher, *OB,* 125. Citing Ignatius, 'Ephesians,' *ANF,* 1:50, 57–58.

[139] Ussher, *OB,* 125. Citing Ignatius, 'Smyrnaeans,' *ANF,* 1:89–92.

Ussher's Ignatian quotations demonstrate that by AD 97 the Ephesian and Smyrnaean churches had bishops that operated alongside the presbytery, but also had some degree of primacy within the presbytery. The expression of this unity may be best captured in the postscript of *The Original*, which states:

> No longer than twelve years after [the writing of Revelation], Ignatius, St. John's scholar, writeth his letters unto the same church. In the beginning whereof, he giveth this testimony unto their bishop: that 'he knew him to have been promoted, not of himself, nor by men, unto that ministry, pertaining to the public weal of the Church', which is every whit as much as if he had called him their angel. Afterwards he telleth them, that there is but 'one bishop', joined 'with the presbytery and the deacons.'[140]

Episcopal primacy is the substance of *The Original*, defending the office of bishop. Here, however, episcopal and presbyteral unity is beginning to emerge in *The Original*, a distinction that will be more fully developed in *The Reduction*. The importance of this unity is evidenced both by the Ignatian material included, but also when considering what Ignatian material is excluded. Perhaps Ignatius' best known statement on the role of a bishop occurs in his letter to the Smyrnaeans: 'wherever the bishop appears, there let the congregation be; just as wherever Jesus Christ is, there is the catholic church.'[141] Concerning these verses, Milton writes, 'What can our church make of these phrases but scandalous[?] ... Excellent *Ignatius!* can ye blame the *Prelates* for making much of this Epistle?'[142]

---

[140] Ussher, *OB*, 146. Citing Ignatius, 'Philadelphians,' *ANF*, 1:79, 81. On the same page, Ussher dates the writing of Revelation 'in the fourteenth year of Domitian, about the ninety-fifth year of our Lord.'

[141] Ignatius, 'Smyrnaeans' in Michael W. Holmes, ed., *The Apostolic Fathers: Greek Texts and English Translations*, 3rd ed. (Grand Rapids: Baker Academic, 2007), 255. I have opted to use Holme's translation rather than the *ANF* in this instance as it more smoothly renders ὅπου ἂν φανῇ ὁ ἐπίσκοπος, ἐκεῖ τὸ πλῆθος ἔστω (Smyrn 8:2). It is beyond the scope of this book to investigate the precise nature of Ignatian episcopacy.

[142] John Milton, *Complete Prose Works*, vol 1., ed. John Cox (New Haven: Yale University Press, 1953), 638. Italics and capitalisation original.

Despite its infamy, Ussher does not include the quotation, instead opting for two quotations that emphasise the unity of the bishop and the presbytery, rather than the necessity of a bishop for a presbytery. There are at least two explanations for this selective use of Ignatius. The first explanation is that he disagreed with that aspect of Ignatius' doctrine of episcopacy, omitting this passage so as not to deter his Presbyterian readers. However, given Ussher's later inclusion of a quotation from Clement that departs from his doctrine of episcopacy, it seems unlikely that he is being deceptively selective in his presentation of source material. The second explanation is that, given Ignatius' previous illustration of a harp, Ussher understood Ignatius' doctrine of episcopacy to be more co-operative than that infamous quotation suggests. If the Archbishop's opening of *The Reduction* is genuine – that he wishes to return to 'that ancient form of government' – that suggests that Ussher did in fact understand his reduced episcopacy to be consonant with Ignatian episcopacy.[143]

Polycarp

As a disciple of the Apostle John, Polycarp's episcopacy provides a strong apologetic for the apostolic origins of bishops. The strength of Polycarp's witness is increased by the volume of preserved early sources to which Ussher had access. Following the pattern of Eusebius, who performed a similar survey in the fourth century, Ussher draws upon Polycarp's own *Letter to the Philippians,* Ignatius' *Epistle to Polycarp,* the anonymous *Martyrdom of Polycarp,* as well as various references in the works of Irenaeus to present a picture of Polycarp's episcopate.[144]

Like his work on Ignatius, Ussher emphasises not only the presence of a bishop over a presbytery, but also the unity of the bishop with the presbytery. He begins by citing Polycarp himself, who opened his epistle with the words, 'Polycarpus and the presbyters that are with him.'[145] Polycarp's epistolary style is often recognised as closely mirroring that of

---

[143] Ussher, 'Reduction,' *WJU,* 12:534.
[144] Polycarp, 'Philippians,' *ANF,* 1:34–36. Ignatius, 'Epistle to Polycarp', *ANF,* 1:93–96. 'The Martyrdom of Polycarp,' *ANF,* 1:39–44. Irenaeus, 'Against Heresies,' *ANF,* 1:416, 563, 568–69.
[145] Ussher, *OB,* 125. Polycarp, 'Philippians,' *ANF,* 1:33.

the biblical epistles.[146] This opening verse, cited by Ussher, is no exception. Just as the Apostle Paul opens most of his epistles with an acknowledgement of his fellow worker Timothy, so Polycarp acknowledges his partnership with the presbytery.[147] As such, like Ignatius, Polycarp acknowledges his primacy as bishop, in that he does not write on behalf of the presbytery. Yet by including the presbytery in his salutation, he expresses a unity with the presbyters of the church that Ussher will seek to replicate in *The Reduction*. This co-operative unity is further evidenced in Polycarp's later chapter on the work and ministry of presbyters where he, in a similar fashion to the Apostle Peter (1 Pet 5:1), refers to himself as a presbyter, not bishop, when speaking of his own ministry.[148]

After identifying Polycarp as a bishop functioning alongside the presbytery, Ussher cites Irenaeus, Eusebius and Polycrates concerning the timing and succession of Polycarp's ministry.[149] Irenaeus is underlined as one who knew 'those worthy men "who succeeded Polycarpus in his see", but also was present when he himself did discourse of his conversation with St John, and of those things which he heard from those who had seen our Lord Jesus.'[150] According to Irenaeus, not only did Polycarp converse with those who had seen Jesus, but was himself 'constituted in Asia bishop of the church which is in Smyrna.'[151] Eusebius is then referenced, as he appears to have had access to the letters of Polycrates, Bishop of Ephesus, who 'lived also in his time and in his neighbourhood, affirming Polycarpus to have been "both bishop and martyr in Smyrna".'[152] In other words; Irenaeus, who knew both Polycarp and his successors, testifies not only to the episcopacy of Polycarp, but the apostolic consecration of Polycarp to the See of Smyrna.

---

[146] Bart Ehrman, 'Introduction to the Letter of Polycarp to the Philippians' in Bart D. Ehrman, ed., *The Apostolic Fathers*, Loeb Classical Library (Cambridge, MA: Harvard University Press, 2003), 324. Holmes, *The Apostolic Fathers*, 273.

[147] 2 Cor 1:1; Phil 1:1; Col 1:1; 1 Thess 1:1; 2 Thess 1:1; Philem 1. cf Rom 16:21. 1 Cor 1:1 has similar opening formula, where Sosthenes is mentioned rather than Timothy.

[148] Polycarp, 'Philippians,' *ANF*, 1:34.

[149] Ussher, *OB*, 126–27.

[150] Ussher, *OB*, 126. Citing Irenaeus, 'Against Heresies,' *ANF*, 1:416, 244.

[151] Ussher, *OB*, 126. Citing Irenaeus, 'Against Heresies,' *ANF*, 1:416.

[152] Ussher, *OB*, 126–27. Citing Polycrates, *Ad Victorem*, in Eusebius, 'Church History,' *NPNF* 2/1:242.

Similar to his postscript treatment of Ignatius, Ussher concludes that, as a result of a synthesis of these ancient sources with Revelation 2:8–11, Polycarp was the angel of the church of Smyrna.[153] Two intertextual observations support Ussher's conclusion. Firstly, both Revelation 2:10 and the *Martyrdom* employ a similar expression in regards to the persecution of the Smyrnaean church.[154] Secondly, both sources refer to the martyrs receiving a crown of immortality.[155] Both of these observations indicate that, at the very least, the author of *The Martyrdom of Polycarp* saw significant overlap between the Smyrnaean's letter in Revelation and their present circumstances.[156] If Ussher is correct concerning the episcopal figure behind the angels of Revelation 2–3, then he is also correct that Polycarp was the angel being addressed in Revelation 2.

Clement

Of the three chief Apostolic Fathers, Ussher devotes the least amount of time to Clement of Rome. Like his presentation of Ignatius and Polycarp, Ussher presents Clement as a bishop in the light of relevant secondary sources: in this instance Tertullian and Irenaeus. In a direct quotation from Tertullian, Ussher states that:

> as the church of Smyrna had Polycarpus placed there by John, and the church of Rome Clement ordained by Peter, so the rest of the churches also did show what bishops they had received by the appointment of the apostles, to traduce the apostolical seed unto them.[157]

Irenaeus, likewise, writes that Clement was 'able to number those whom by the apostles were ordained bishops in the churches, and their successors unto our days.'[158] Ussher summarises that Clement, 'did both see the apostles and conferred with them', proving 'the succession of the bishops of Rome.'[159]

---

[153] Ussher, *OB*, 126.
[154] Lightfoot, *The Apostolic Fathers*, 185–87.
[155] Unknown Author, 'The Martyrdom of Polycarp,' *ANF*, 1:42. Rev 2:10.
[156] Unknown Author, 'The Martyrdom of Polycarp,' *ANF*, 1:43
[157] Ussher, *OB*, 127. Tertullian, 'Prescription Against Heretics,' *ANF*, 3:258.
[158] Irenaeus, 'Against Heresies,' *ANF*, 1:415.
[159] Ussher, *OB*, 127.

Like Ussher's Old Testament defence of episcopacy, Clement of Rome correlates the ministry of Old Testament priests and Levites with presbyters and deacons.[160] However, Ussher does not cite this correlation, neither here in his historical defence, nor previously in his biblical defence. Rather than employ Clement on the origins of episcopacy, Ussher engages Clement on the functions of episcopacy. Ussher begins his use of Clement by recording that the Corinthian church, to whom Clement wrote, was a fractious group. He goes on to provide a very short quotation from Clement on the role of the bishop in the settling of disputes, while providing the fuller Clementine quotation in a footnote.[161] The brief use of Clement, the contextual comment, and the relegation of the fuller quotation to a footnote, suggests that Ussher is using Clement cautiously. The quotation in the footnote reveals that Clement understood episcopacy as given by divine revelation, with the apostles having 'obtained perfect fore-knowledge' of the appointment of bishops over the church.[162] This view of the office and origin of episcopacy is higher than Ussher's, which may explain why Clement, though chronologically closest to the New Testament authors, is employed last and least of the Apostolic Fathers.

Conclusion

This chapter's brief survey of Ussher's use of the Apostolic Fathers has synthesised his argument both logically and chronologically. In doing so, it has demonstrated Ussher's own method concerning the Apostolic Fathers. In each instance, he established the historicity of the Father's episcopacy from relevant sources, before using their own works to determine their position regarding either their own episcopacy or the nature of episcopacy in general. In this section of *The Original*, the shoots of Ussher's reduced episcopacy – the central, but cooperative leadership of a bishop with his presbytery – begin to emerge. Both Ford and Snoddy conclude that if one agrees with Ussher's principle that the early church provides the purest model of ecclesiastical government, then both Ussher's claim and method bear careful consideration.[163] Ussher's historical defence persuasively presents the presence of a distinct presbytery and episcopacy in the earliest years of the church. However,

---

[160] Ussher, *OB*, 118–119. Clement, 'First Corinthians,' *ANF*, 1:16.

[161] Ussher, *OB*, 128.

[162] Clement, 'First Corinthians,' *ANF*, 1:17.

[163] Ford, *James Ussher*, 241. Snoddy, 'Introduction,' in *James Ussher*, xxxiii.

his selective use of Ignatius and Clement does raise the question as to whether the episcopacies of the Apostolic Fathers were quite as cooperative as Ussher suggests.

CHAPTER 5

REVIVING THE ANCIENT FORM

Ussher's *The Reduction of Episcopacie* was first published as a pamphlet in the year of his death (1656), and again one year later as part of a larger collection of work.[164] The latter edition begins with a preface to *The Reduction,* written by Ussher's former chaplain and editor of the collected work, Nicholas Bernard. These prefatory notes reveal that the second edition came directly from Ussher's 'own hand', taking into account Ussher's own marginalia, presumably from the first publication, before he died.[165] This chapter will be considering the later, expanded edition, as found in Snoddy's *James Ussher and a Reformed Episcopal Church.*[166]

Context and production

Aside from Bernard's prefatory notes, there is very little external evidence surrounding the composition of *The Reduction.* Several proposals have been made: that it was both penned and published in 1641; that it was brought to a House of Lords' committee but later withdrawn; that it was published in 1648 in relation to a settlement on the Isle of Wight; or that it remained hidden until Ussher's death.[167] Given the reference within

---

[164] Ussher, *The Reduction of Episcopacie unto the Form of Synodical Government Received in the Antient Church: Proposed as an Expedient for the compremising of the now Differences, and preventing of those Troubles that may arise about the matter of Church-Government.* (London: T.N. for G.B. and T.C., 1656). Nicholas Bernard, ed., *the Judgement of the Late Arch-Bishop of Armagh, and Primate of Ireland,* 1. *Of the Extent of Christs death, and satisfaction, &c.* (London: n.p., 1657.)

[165] Ussher, 'Reduction,' *WJU,* 12:529

[166] Ussher, 'The Reduction of Episcopacy' in Snoddy, *James Ussher,* 148–54. Also available in *WJU,* 12:531–536.

[167] J. C. Spalding and M. F. Brass, 'Reduction of the Episcopacy as a Means to Unity in England, 1640–1662,' *Church History* 30 (1961): 417; Elizabethanne Boran, '"Propagating Religion and Endeavoring the Reformation of the Whole World": Irish Bishops and the Hartlib Circle in the Mid Seventeenth Century' in V. P. Carey and Ute Lotz-Heumann, eds., *Taking Sides? Colonial and Confessional Mentalities in Early Modern Ireland* (Dublin: Irish Academic Press, 2003), 181; W. M. Abbott, 'James Ussher and "Ussherian" Episcopacy, 1640–1656: The Primate and His Reduction Manuscript', *Albion* 22 (1990): 237–59; Richard Baxter, *Reliquiae Baxterianæ* (1696), 1:238; J. A. Carr, *The Life and*

The Reduction to the Triennial Act that was passed by the Long Parliament on 15 February, 1641, alongside Bernard's editorial work, it seems most likely that a manuscript copy was produced and circulated privately by Ussher sometime after the middle of February 1641, before being published in 1656.[168] The delay in publication is perhaps best explained by Charles I's speech at Whitehall in January, 1641, warning against any petitions on Church government that deviated from 'the purest Times of Queen Elizabeth's Days', or that rendered bishops as 'no better that Cyphers.'[169]

The ongoing ecclesiastical debates that marked the first eight months of the Long Parliament have played a significant role in the reading and interpretation of *The Reduction*.[170] This polarised political setting, compounded by the breadth of Ussher's friendships and influence, has led to *The Reduction* being considered a failed *via media* between two ecclesiastical poles.[171] Ussher's conciliatory intent is evident in *The Reduction's* subtitle: 'an expedient for the prevention of these troubles, which afterwards did arise about the matter of church government.'[172] Likewise, the first subheading of *The Reduction* reads: 'Episcopal and Presbyterial Government conjoined.'[173] In 1679, *The Reduction* was even republished under that title.[174] Is this proof of Ussher's 'prescopalian' convictions or intent? It is evident that Ussher sought to reconcile the episcopal and Presbyterian factions of the Church of England. However, this chapter will seek to demonstrate that, despite first appearances, 'prescopalian' is a poor summary of *The Reduction,* as Ussher was not seeking to presbyterianise the Church of England.

Times of James Ussher Archbishop of Armagh (London: Gardner, Darton, 1895), 271; Hugh Trevor-Roper, *Catholics, Anglicans and Puritans: 17th Century Essays,* (Oxford: Oxford University Press, 1987), 151. Ford, *James Ussher,* 246.

[168] Ford, *James Ussher,* 246.

[169] *Journal of the House of Lords: Vol IV,* 1629–42 (London: n.p., 1771), 142. Cited in Snoddy, 'Introduction,' *James Ussher,* xxxvi.

[170] Richard Cust, 'The Defence of Episcopacy on the Eve of Civil War: Jeremy Taylor and the Rutland Petition of 1641,' *Journal of Ecclesiastical History* 61, no. 1 (January 2017), 65. Spalding and Brass, 'Reduction of the Episcopacy,' 416.

[171] Ford, *James Ussher,* 250.

[172] Ussher, 'Reduction,' 148.

[173] Ussher, 'Reduction,' 149.

[174] Ussher, *Episcopal and Presbyterial Government Conjoyned* (London: n.p., 1769; Edinburgh: n.p., 1689, 1703, 1706). See Snoddy, *James Ussher,* 148.

Episcopal and Presbyterial government conjoined

So far, this study has used the label Presbyterian to reference the dual convictions that individual congregations ought to be ruled by a plurality of elders, and that the wider church ought to be governed by a presbytery comprised of elders from each of those congregations.[175] Opinions vary on whether the 'established' Presbyterian church of 1646 was 'something other than Presbyterian', but that debate is beyond the scope of this study.[176] Ussher's use of presbyterial here, as evidenced by his four-step programme of reform, is only concerned with the governance of the wider church, not an individual congregation. Nowhere in *The Reduction,* or elsewhere in his works, does he address the legitimacy of the office of 'ruling elders', nor the necessity of their presence in each congregation. As in *The Original,* Ussher will present the case for an episcopal government that works alongside the presbyters of the rural deaneries, the diocese and the national church. Ussher's use of 'Presbyterial Government' in the heading should not, therefore, be conflated with Presbyterian government.[177]

The Ordinal

The opening paragraph of *The Reduction* suggests that Ussher understood his position to be found within the 1559 *Ordinal* itself. He begins by quoting from the charge given to priests at their ordination, stating that 'By order of the Church of England, all presbyters are charged "to administer the doctrine and sacraments, and the discipline of Christ, as the Lord hath commanded, and as this realm has received the same."'[178] In other words, the priests are charged, like bishops, to administer church discipline. Ussher's only departure from the *Ordinal* is the use of 'presbyter' rather than 'priest'. This may reflect an attempt to appeal to his readers who opposed the term 'priest'. However, the use

---

[175] *WCF,* 'The Form of Presbyterial Church Government,' 599.
[176] Robert Baillie, *The Letters and Journals of Robert Baillie,* ed. David Laing, 3 vols. (Edinburgh: Bannatyne Club, 1841–43), vol. 2, 362. Laurence Kaplan, 'English Civil War Politics and the Religious Settlement,' *Church History* 41:3 (September 1972): 307.
[177] Ussher, 'Reduction,' 149.
[178] Ussher, 'Reduction,' 149. 'The Form of Ordering Priests' (1559) in William Keating Clay, ed., *Liturgical Services: Liturgies and Occasional Forms of Prayer Set Forth in the Reign of Queen Elizabeth* (Cambridge: Parker Society, 1847), 290.

of presbyter rather than priest is typical of Ussher's writing, perhaps due to the ongoing presence of the Roman priests in his native Ireland.

After highlighting the disciplinary authority given to presbyters at their ordination, Ussher goes on to remind his readers of the scriptural text that opens the service, and one particular verse in that text: 'Take heed unto your selves, and to all the flock among whom the Holy Ghost hath made you overseers to rule the congregation of God, which he hath purchased with his blood.'[179] The highlighting of Acts 20:28 is notable, not least because it was the key text for those, like Ussher and Cranmer before him, who held to the synonymity of presbyters and bishops in the biblical texts.[180] Indeed, the episcopal and presbyterial cooperation that Ussher will present, may be little more than an attempt to express this synonymity as it is found in the Biblical texts. Ussher's use of the *Ordinal* in the opening paragraph of *The Reduction* demonstrates that the reduced episcopacy he was advocating was not, in Ussher's mind, a departure from or a softening of 'Anglican' ecclesiastics, but rather an outworking of the earliest formularies of the reformed English church.

Ussher's attempts to 'reduce' the English episcopate ultimately failed, not least because of the royal and political incompetence. According to Ford, 'royal stubbornness and ineptitude', meant that, 'when Ussher's proposal had the best opportunity for widespread acceptance, in 1641, Charles rejected it, and when it had little hope of success, in 1648, he endorsed it.'[181] Despite its failure to achieve the outcomes the archbishop hoped for, there are some hints that the substance of his argument adversely affected later confessional revisions. Twenty years after *The Reduction* was written, following the Great Restoration, the Convocation of Canterbury and York made some subtle changes to the *Ordinal*. Where the 1550, 1552 and 1559 versions of the *Ordinal* had included Acts 20 in 'The form of ordering Priests', the Convocations of 1662 removed that reading from the priesting service and inserted it into 'The Consecration of Archbishops and Bishops'.[182] Similarly, they inserted the words

---

[179] Ussher, 'Reduction,' 149. Cf Acts 20:28.
[180] Ussher, *OB*, 120–21. Cranmer, 'Questions and Answers' in Cox, *Miscellaneous Writing and Letters*, 117.
[181] Ford, *James Ussher*, 255.
[182] *The First and Second Prayer Books of Edward VI*, Everyman's Library (London: J. M. Dent & Sons, 1910), 303, 449. Clay, *Liturgical services*, 284. 284. *The Book of Common Prayer and Administration of the Sacraments* (Cambridge: CUP, 2004), 584.

'ordaining' and 'ordained' into the title and presentation of the 'The Form of Consecrating of an Archbishop or Bishop'. Previously, the *Ordinal* only had the words 'consecration' or 'consecrated' in the respective title and presentation.[183] Both revisions contribute to the removal of presbyterial and episcopal synonymity from the 1662 *Ordinal*. Given the wide circulation of *The Reduction* in the 1650s, it is highly likely that his arguments for the synonymity of presbyters and bishops were a significant factor in the Convocation's changes to the post-restoration *Ordinal*.

This ancient form of government

Having presented the consonance of his position with the *Ordinal*, Ussher goes on to provide a succinct summary of the historiographical argument for episcopal oversight. Tracing a familiar argument from *The Original* concerning the angels in the biblical book of Revelation, Ussher identifies the 'angel of the Church in Ephesus' as the 'one president' who ruled over the other presbyters of the church.[184] The language of president would have been familiar, and perhaps even favourable, to those on the Presbyterian end of the political and ecclesiastical divide, given that the reformed churches of Holland, Switzerland and France used a presbyterial system with a synodically elected president.[185] Calvin himself, almost one hundred years previously, conceded that there 'is no meeting of the Senate without a consul ... no association without a president. Thus there would be nothing absurd in our confessing that the apostles yielded primacy of this sort to Peter.'[186] The presence of 'president', used three times in this short document, as well as his later concession regarding superintendency, may be indicative of the political acuity of *The Reduction*: the willingness to concede terminology in the pursuit of the greater goal of uniting the divided parties.[187]

Whereas *The Original* was primarily concerned with the existence of episcopal figures in the early church, *The Reduction* is focused primarily on the nature of their leadership. In two short paragraphs, Ussher cites

---

[183] *The First and Second Prayer Books of Edward VI*, 313, 459. Clay, *Liturgical services*, 293. *The Book of Common Prayer*, 584, 588.

[184] Ussher, 'Reduction,' 150. Ussher, *OB*, 121–123, 132, 145.

[185] Wolfe, 'Introduction,' in Bush, *Complete Prose Works of John Milton*, vol. 1, 198.

[186] Calvin, *Institutes*, IV.6.8.

[187] Ussher, 'Reduction,' 150.

seven sources in chronological order, starting with Ignatius and ending with English canon law. As with *The Original,* Ignatius is employed to argue for the 'harmonious consent' of a bishop's leadership with the presbytery.[188] This harmony, Ussher argues, is expressed by the Apostle Paul in his record of the presbyters laying their hands on Timothy (I Tim 4:14).[189] For Ussher, the laying on of hands is not a record of Timothy's ordination to the presbyterate, but rather his consecration to the episcopate by his fellow presbyters.

Ussher then cites a long quote from Tertullian, himself using the language of 'præsident' to refer to those 'certain approved elders, who have obtained this honour not by reward, but by good report'.[190] The same office is referred to in a later work by Tertullian as the *summus sacerdos,* with the full reference, provided by Ussher in his footnotes: 'the chief priest, who is the bishop, has, of course, the right of conferring baptism, then the presbyters and deacons.'[191] This quotation, while giving the bishop primacy in the administration of baptism, is understood by Ussher to communicate that the 'rest of the dispensers of the Word and sacraments [were] joined in the common government of the church.'[192] Ussher presents a similar structure in the writings of Cornelius, Bishop of Rome, who wrote to Cyprian of his 'gathering together the presbytery' in response to the return of the Confessors to his church.[193] Cyprian likewise is cited as referring to '"to the flourishing clergy which there did preside", or rule "with him".'[194] Ussher finds this mode of government supported again in the fourth Council of Carthage, which stated that 'the bishop might hear no man's cause without the presence of the clergy: and that otherwise the bishop's sentence should be void, unless it were confirmed by the presence of the clergy.'[195] This united government found favour with the Saxon Bishop Egbert of York (d. AD 766), who inserted it into English canon law.[196]

---

[188] Ussher, 'Reduction,' 150. Ignatius, 'Ephesians,' *ANF,* 1:50–51.

[189] Ussher, 'Reduction,' 150.

[190] Ussher, 'Reduction,' 150. Tertullian, 'Apology,' *ANF,* 3:46; *PL,* 1:469A.

[191] Ussher, 'Reduction,' 150. Translation by Snoddy. Tertullian, 'On Baptism,' *ANF,* 3:677; *PL,* 1:951A.

[192] Ussher, 'Reduction,' 151.

[193] Ussher, 'Reduction,' 151. Cornelius, 'to Cyprian,' *ANF,* 5:323.

[194] Ussher, 'Reduction,' 151.

[195] Ussher, 'Reduction,' 151. *PL,* 84:202B.

[196] Ussher, 'Reduction,' 151. *PL,* 187:987A.

Ussher concludes this section by lamenting that 'this kind of presbyterial government hath long been disused' in the Church of England. According to Ussher, this disuse was not inherent to the essence of the Church of England's ecclesial system, but rather it came about 'only from the custom now received in this realm.'[197] The conventional title of rector, according to Ussher, 'professeth that every pastor hath a right to rule the church ... and to administer the discipline of Christ', thus again demonstrating that Ussher's position is not an innovation.[198] Despite its long disuse, Ussher asserts 'how easily this ancient form of government by the united suffrages of the clergy might be revived again, and with what little shew of alteration the synodical conventions of the pastors of every parish might be accorded with the presidency of the bishops.'[199] Finally, he offers four propositions of synodical restructure, tiered from the parochial to provincial church. The fourth proposition only concerns the administration of the provincial synods, so we will focus on the first three.

Pastoral and parochial discipline

Ussher's first point suggests a weekly meeting of the rector with the church wardens to 'take notice of such as live scandalously in that congregation, who are to receive such several admonitions and reproofs, as the quality of their offence shall observe.'[200] Given the plurality of leadership involved, this model of congregational ministry may well have appealed to Ussher's Presbyterian readers. However, the role given to the wardens by Ussher is little more than an extension of the authority given them in 1604 canon law. Canons CXV to CXVIII instruct the biannual presentation of 'Criminal persons, ... said Delinquents or their Friends' to the diocesan bishop by the vicar and churchwardens.[201] Ussher's first proposal, then, is not a radical departure from the Church of England's canon law. Rather, he is merely proposing an extra step in the disciplinary procedure, allowing the presbyter to administer discipline to the recusant before bringing them to the bishop, should they remain unrepentant. Although not radical in nature, this first step is indicative of the more radical changes that Ussher will proceed to suggest.

[197] Ussher, 'Reduction,' 151.
[198] Ussher, 'Reduction,' 151.
[199] Ussher, 'Reduction,' 151.
[200] Ussher, 'Reduction,' 152.
[201] 'The Canons of 1603 (1604)' in Gerald Bray, ed., *The Anglican Canons 1529–1947* (Woodbridge, Suffolk: Boydell & Brewer, 1998), 415.

Chorepiscopacy

The second point moves from the parochial level to the rural deanery and represents the most radical position of Ussher's four propositions. Here, Ussher suggests that rather than the number of suffragan bishops being limited by a Henrician decree, the number 'might very well be conformed unto the number of rural deaneries, into which every diocese is subdivided.'[202] In this structure, the suffragan bishops would then become *chorepiscopoi*, assembling monthly synods to 'conclude all matters that shall be brought into debate before them.'[203] These *chorepiscopi* were, according to Elrington, the only aspect of *The Reduction* that differed from a Presbyterian polity, causing him to wonder if *The Reduction* 'had not received some pruning from the antiepiscopal prepossessions of Dr Bernard.'[204] Elrington understood *chorepiscopoi* to be bishops with 'all power of order and jurisdiction' taken from them, left with nothing but 'the empty title of superintendent or president of the ecclesiastical synod.'[205]

The problem of an Ussherian definition of chorepiscopacy is multiplied by the sparsity of reference to the office in his works. Only once does he define chorepiscopacy – and there he does so tentatively. His historical work on ninth-century Celtic ministry (*Of The Original And First Institution Of Corbes, Herenaches, And Termon Lands*), provisionally states that 'the chorepiscopus seemeth to me to have his original from the same with archipresbyter.'[206] Given that the office of rural dean finds its origins in the title archipresbyter, and Cranmer's proposal that each deanery ought to have a 'rural Archpresbyter' appointed yearly by the bishop, it is easy to see how Elrington understood chorepiscopacy as no episcopacy at all.[207] However, an examination of the role of the *chorepiscopoi* in the fourth century may shed some light on Ussher's

---

[202] *The Statutes: Revised Edition*, vol. 1., Henry III to James II, A.D. 1235/6–1685 (London: Eyre and Spottiswoode, 1870), 447–49, 578. Snoddy, *James Ussher and Reformed Episcopal Church*, 152. *WJU*, 12:534.

[203] Ussher, 'Reduction,' 152.

[204] Elrington, 'The Life of James Ussher,' *WJU*, 1:209.

[205] Elrington, 'The Life of James Ussher,' *WJU*, 1:209.

[206] Ussher, 'Reduction,' *WJU*, 11:419–45, 430–31.

[207] E. R. Massey, 'Rural Dean' in George Harford and Morley Stevenson, eds., *The Prayer Book Dictionary* (New York: Longmans, Green, & Co., 1912), 772. Cranmer, 'Reformatio Legum Ecclesiasticarum,' in Bray, *Tudor Church Reform*, 350–53. Elrington, 'The Life of James Ussher,' *WJU*, 1:209.

understanding of their authority. Both the Synod of Ancyra (314) and the Synod of Antioch (341) decreed that *chorepiscopoi* had no right to ordain presbyters and deacons without letters from the bishop.[208] Towards the end of the fourth century, the Synod of Laodicea (380) replaced the chorepiscopal office with the office of *periodeutes*, who functioned similarly to a modern day archdeacon.[209] That these synods forbade *chorepiscopoi* from ordaining without dimissory letters suggests that until those decrees, they were performing ordinations without them. It is likely, then, that for Ussher, who ostensibly held to the principle that the earliest models 'provided the purest model for the contemporary church', that these *chorepiscopoi* would have had the authority both to ordain and to discipline.[210]

In summary, Ussher's second proposal is that the number of suffragans ought to correlate to the number of rural deaneries across the Church of England.[211] These suffragans, similar to the *chorepiscopoi* of antiquity, would hold a monthly synod with the rectors and incumbents of the parishes, to 'conclude all matters that shall be brought into debate before them'.[212] *Contra* Elrington, Ussher's parallel with *chorepiscopoi* does not relegate these suffragans to a sub-episcopal office.[213]

Bishops or superintendents?

Ussher's third proposition addresses diocesan synods, to be held 'once or twice in the year, as it should be thought most convenient.'[214] As with the previous two propositions, should a matter remain unresolved, it would pass to the next provincial or national synod. Perhaps the most significant aspect of this third proposition is Ussher's famous concession regarding terminology. Here, he writes, concerning the governing of the synod, 'all things might be concluded by the bishop, or superintendent, call him

---

[208] Michael Ott, 'Chorepiscopi' in Charles G. Herberman et al., eds., *The Catholic Encyclopedia,* vol. 16 (New York: The Encyclopedia Press, 1914), 24–25. 'Synod of Ancyra,' Canon XIII, *NPNF* 2/14:69. 'Synod of Antioch,' Canon VIII, *NPNF* 2/4:112.

[209] Ott, 'Chorepiscopi' in Herberman, *Catholic Encyclopedia,* 25. Synod of Laodicea, Canon LVII, *NPNF* 2/14:158.

[210] Ford, *James Ussher,* 241.

[211] *The Statutes: Revised Edition,* vol. 1, 447–49, 578. Snoddy, *James Ussher,* 152.

[212] Ussher, 'Reduction,' 152.

[213] Elrington, 'The Life of James Ussher,' *WJU,* 1:209.

[214] Ussher, 'Reduction,' 153.

whether you will.'[215] As noted above, Elrington understands there to be a sharp distinction between the office of bishop and the superintendents of the Swiss reformed churches, suggesting that Ussher was making a momentary concession 'produced upon his gentle nature by the violent commotion which he witnessed.'[216] However, given that Ussher was writing *The Original,* which argues strongly for the biblical and apostolic witness to the office of episcopacy, at the same time that he was writing *The Reduction,* it seems unlikely that he would make a concession of substance in one document that he was explicitly writing against in another. Ussher's concession, then, is better understood as a purely terminological one, because, particularly in light of the tempestuous political climate of the 1640s, the function of the office was more important than the name of the office.[217]

Conclusion

The Reduction represented what Ford called a 'dramatic reinterpretation of the ecclesiology of the English church.'[218] It was no Laudian episcopacy, casting doubt on the status and ordinations of non-episcopal churches. Neither was it, however, a return to the moderate Calvinist episcopacy of the Edwardian and Elizabethan divines.[219] It was, rather, an attempt to return to the harmonious governance of bishop and presbyter that Ussher saw in both the New Testament and the early church.[220] Ussher understood his position to be consonant not just with the New Testament and the early church, but also with the Church of England's 1559 *Ordinal.*

It is difficult, then, to define *The Reduction* as prescopalian. It is beyond doubt that Ussher was seeking to convince those with Presbyterian convictions within the Church of England of the legitimacy of his position. The subtitle of *The Reduction* concerning the conjoining of the two modes of government, and the use of 'superintendent' reveals this

---

[215] Ussher, 'Reduction,' 153.
[216] Elrington, *WJU,* 1:209–10.
[217] Snoddy, 'Introduction,' *James Ussher,* xxxiv.
[218] Ford, *James Ussher,* 241.
[219] Anthony Milton, *Catholic and Reformed: The Roman and Protestant Churches in English Protestant Thought, 1600–1640* (Cambridge: CUP, 1994), 466–67. Ford, *James Ussher,* 241.
[220] Ussher, *OB,* 125; Ussher, 'Reduction,' 150–51. Ignatius, 'Ephesians,' *ANF,* 1:50, 57–58.

conciliatory and persuasive intent. However, Ussher's suffragan structures were not English versions of Scottish presbyteries.[221] His identification of suffragans as *chorepiscopoi* suggests that he was not removing authority from episcopal officers. Indeed, this work of Ussher was never titled *The Removal of Episcopacy,* but *The Reduction of Episcopacy.* Although others, even in his own time, interpret Ussher's position as a limitation of episcopal authority, Ussher's *Reduction* is better understood as a *reducere:* a return to the ancient form.

---

[221] *Contra* Elrington, 'The Life of James Ussher,' *WJU,* 1:209.

CONCLUSION

Was Archbishop Ussher a 'prescopalian?' In order to determine whether this designation of the archbishop holds, this study has surveyed relevant details of his life and ministry in the Church of Ireland, as well as his two works directly concerned with ecclesiastical government: *The Original of Bishops and Metropolitans,* and *The Reduction of Episcopacy.*

Chapter one demonstrated that the commingling of Presbyterians and episcopalians in the Church of Ireland was not initiated by Ussher, but inherited from his episcopal predecessors. Chapter two outlined Ussher's argument for episcopal origins in the Old Testament. Chapter three presented the archbishop's evidence for the continuation of that Old Testament structure into the New Testament church. Chapter four presented Ussher's proofs for the presence of episcopal figures from the earliest days of the church. Finally, chapter five argued that *The Reduction* was not a compromise between Presbyterianism and episcopalianism, but rather a manifesto to reform the Church of England's ecclesiastical structures to the ancient form of the first- and second-century church.

A large proportion of this study has been devoted to Ussher's exegesis of both the Scriptures and the early church fathers. This is important for three reasons. First, Ussher himself asserts that his episcopal precepts were derived from the Old Testament, the New Testament and the adoption of episcopacy in the early church. Secondly, only by a detailed examination of the archbishop's exegesis does the ingenuity of his approach becomes apparent. Thirdly, and most importantly for our discussion, Ussher's exegesis of Scripture enables us to evaluate whether his position could rightly be labelled 'prescopalian'. This survey has concluded that while Ussher consistently pursued theological and ecclesiastical reform in both the English and Irish church, he was neither a convictional 'prescopalian' nor *en route* to becoming one.

Ussher's scholarly status, his consistent pursuit of reform, and his popularity across the ecclesiastical divides of seventeenth-century England made him the perfect candidate to produce a halfway house between Presbyterianism and episcopalianism. However, *The Reduction* was not a promotion of Presbyterian government.[222] Rather, it proposed to allow presbyters to exercise the authority given them in the *Ordinal*, and to unite them, like strings to a harp, with their suffragan bishop. A Presbyterian may have interpreted *The Reduction* as a step in the right direction, as evidenced by Robert Baillie's letters.[223] Baillie himself was more moderate than many of his Scottish brethren, in that while he desired episcopacy to be removed, he did not think it ought to be abjured, given that the continental reformers had not done so.[224] However, despite Baillie's designation of Ussher's position as a 'limited good and ... calked Episcopacie' he nonetheless hoped that Ussher's plans would not 'thryve in any of their designes.'[225] Baillie's rejection of Ussher's episcopacy reveals that, despite the protestations of later interpreters, Ussher's reduced episcopacy was not a compromised concession to his Presbyterian neighbours.

Whereas older scholarship misunderstood Ussher as 'prescopalian', this study has argued that the archbishop was a committed and convinced episcopalian. As an Irish Calvinist regularly pursuing theological and ecclesiastical reform, Ussher was undoubtedly a 'hotter sort' of protestant when compared with his Laudian colleagues.[226] His ecclesiastical reform, however, was no call to upend episcopacy 'root and branch'. Rather, he desired to both demonstrate the biblical and historical grounds of episcopacy – present though overgrown in the English church – and to see it reduced to its scriptural and ancient form. It would be a government, as Ussher himself says, 'according to the word of God and the practice of the ancient church.'[227]

---

[222] *Contra* Ford, 'Everywhere, Always, By All,' 95.

[223] Baillie, *Letters and Journals of Robert Baillie*, vol. 1, 287.

[224] Alexander D. Campbell, Episcopacy in the Mind of Robert Baillie, 1637–1662, *The Scottish Historical Review* Volume XCIII, 1: No. 236: (April 2014). 37.

[225] Robert Baillie, 'to the Presbytery of Irvine,' in *Letters and Journals of Robert Baillie*, vol. 1, 287.

[226] John Spurr, *English Puritanism 1603–1689* (New York: Palgrave Macmillan, 1998), 1.

[227] Ussher, 'Reduction,' *WJU*, 12:536.

EPILOGUE

EPISCOPACY TODAY

Having presented this study to the Latimer Trust for publication, I was encouraged to offer a few final contemporary application points. This presented perhaps the most daunting part of the booklet for at least two reasons. Firstly, my own experience of ordained Anglican ministry is limited to two parishes, two hemispheres apart, neither of which lies within the Church of England. Secondly, although there is nothing new under the sun (Ecclesiastes 1:9), the current tensions in the global Anglican communion, not least surrounding the consecration and jurisdiction of Bishops, makes drawing contemporary applications particularly difficult.

With that being said, I ask the reader to allow me to tentatively suggest two applications of Ussher's works.

For priests and deacons: do not despise episcopacy

Ussher's *The Original of Bishops and Metropolitans* is ultimately an exposition of the preface of the *Ordinal*: 'It is evident unto all men diligently reading holy Scripture and ancient authors, that from the Apostles' time there have been these Orders of Ministers in Christ's Church; Bishops, Priests, and Deacons.'[228] Despite the *Ordinal*'s assertion that these offices are not simply historical but biblical, evangelical Anglicans have neglected, downplayed and sometimes denied the veracity of the office of bishop.

In his helpful booklet on Ussher's ecclesiology, Wallace Benn suggests several reasons for this neglect, including an ignorance of history, or experiences with difficult bishops.[229] To his list of reasons one might add the rise in interdenominational partnerships and the decline of evangelical representation within the House of Bishops. This downplaying can be seen when ministry within the Church of England is commended because it is, or at least has been, the 'best boat to fish

---

[228] *The Book of Common Prayer*, 553.
[229] Wallace Benn, *Usher on Bishops: A Reforming Ecclesiology* (Sheffield: Mensa, 2002), 9.

from'. However, if an evangelical minister must cross their fingers at their ordination or institution, on what grounds can they oppose other bishops, priests and deacons who likewise have crossed their fingers when they vow to 'banish and drive away all erroneous and strange doctrines contrary to God's Word'?[230]

Ussher's ecclesiastical retrieval and reform ought to give such evangelical Anglicans pause. Here we find a robust biblical and historical defence and application of episcopal oversight. Here, we find a compelling argument that episcopacy is not simply one of many valid forms of church government, rather it is the most faithful form of Church government. Rather than downplay – or worse, deny – the validity of episcopal oversight, the evangelical Anglican can, with Ussher, celebrate the biblical validity of their church government. Moreover then, as convictional episcopalians, they can call on their Bishops to faithfully and diligently 'banish and drive away all erroneous and strange doctrine contrary to God's Word', as they promised at their consecration.[231]

Other forms of church government, propounded by godly men and women in England and around the world, may have pragmatic or cultural benefits, but the system of government attested to in the Scriptures and practised by the earliest Christians remains the best way to organise the body of Christ.

For bishops: remember priests are your partners in godly discipline

Perhaps the most radical aspect of Ussher's *The Reduction* was the call to multiply the number of bishops within the Church of England. This increase in the quantity of bishops both served to place bishops closer to the life of the local church and to work in closer partnership with the priests of the dioceses and deaneries. For Ussher, a bishop is not a master to be served, dispatching orders from the comfort of the See House, but rather a fellow worker in the harvest.

Given the historical, political and social status of the office of bishop, it should be no surprise that a bishop, perhaps more so than most, may be tempted to lord it over others. This temptation arose within the apostles, when they squabbled among themselves regarding who was the greatest (Mark 10:35–41). The Lord Jesus commanded them not to lord their status

---

[230] 'The Form and Manner of Ordering of Priests,' *The Book of Common Prayer,* 569.
[231] *The Book of Common Prayer,* 591.

over others, but rather, following his own example, to serve: 'whoever would be first among you must be slave of all. For even the Son of Man came not to be served but to serve, and to give his life as a ransom for many' (Mark 10:44–45).

Ussher's exposition of the leadership structures of the people of God, in both the Old Testament, the New Testament and the early church, ought to encourage bishops to think rightly of themselves. They are both partners and pastors of the priests in their diocese. This partnership is evident in the *Ordinal* itself: both Bishops and Priests are commended to be ready 'with all faithful diligence, to banish and drive away all erroneous and strange doctrines contrary to God's Word.'[232] As in the *Ordinal,* Ussher's emphasis is on the discipline of those promoting erroneous doctrine and ungodliness, either in the local church or the wider diocese. Bishops, then, are not to be simply ecclesiastical estate agents, nor chief administrators; rather they are to be shepherds, exercising godly oversight over the church, bought with Christ's own blood (Acts 20:28).

---

[232] *The Book of Common Prayer,* 576, 591.

BIBLIOGRAPHY

Abbott, W. M. 'James Ussher and "Ussherian" Episcopacy, 1640–1656: The Primate and His Reduction Manuscript,' *Albion* 22 (1990): 237–59.

Baillie, Robert. *The Letters and Journals of Robert Baillie.* Edited by David Laing. 3 vols. Edinburgh: Bannatyne Club, 1841–43.

Baxter, Richard. *Reliquiæ Baxterianæ.* London: n.p., 1696.

Benn, Wallace. *Usher on Bishops: A Reforming Ecclesiology.* Sheffield: Mensa, 2002.

Bernard, Nicholas, ed. *The Judgement of the Late Arch-Bishop of Armagh, and Primate of Ireland, 1. Of the Extent of Christs death, and satisfaction, &c.* London: n.p., 1657.

Beza, Theodore. *Annotationes Maiores in Novum DN. Nostri Iesu Christi Testamentum.* 2 vols. Geneva, 1594.

Beza, Theodore. *Tractatus pius et moderatus de vera Excommunicatione, et christiano Presbyterio.* Geneva: Jean Le Preux, 1590.

Bilson, Thomas. *The Perpetual Government of Christ's Church.* London: Christopher Barker, 1593.

Bray, Gerald, ed. *The Anglican Canons 1529–1947.* Woodbridge, Suffolk: Boydell & Brewer, 1998.

Bray, Gerald, ed. *Tudor Church Reform: The Henrician Canons of 1535 and the Reformatio Legum Ecclesiasticarum.* Woodbridge, Suffolk: Boydell & Brewer, 2000.

Bridges, John, *A Defence of the Governement Established in the Church of Englande for Ecclesiasticall Matters.* London: John Windet, 1587.

Brightman, Thomas. *A Revelation of the Apocalyps.* Amsterdam: Thomas Stafford, 1611.

Bullinger, Heinrich. *A Hundred Sermons vpo the Apocalips of Jesu Christe.* Translated by John Daus. London: Iohn Daus, 1561.

Bush, Douglas, et al., eds. *The Complete Prose Works of John Milton.* 6 vols. New Haven: Yale University Press, 1953–73.

Calvin, John. *Commentary on the Book of the Prophet Isaiah.* Translated by William Pringle. 4 vols. Grand Rapids: Eerdmans, 1956.

Calvin, John. *Institutes of the Christian Religion*. Translated by Ford Lewis Battles. Edited by John T. McNeill. Louisville: Westminster John Knox Press, 1960.

Campbell, Alexander D., 'Episcopacy in the Mind of Robert Baillie, 1637–1662,' *The Scottish Review Journal* Volume XCIII, 1: No. 236: April 2014, 29–55.

Carey, V. P., and Ute Lotz-Heumann, eds. *Taking Sides? Colonial and Confessional Mentalities in Early Modern Ireland*. Dublin: Irish Academic Press, 2003.

Cargill Thompson, W. D. J., 'A Reconsideration of Richard Bancroft's Paul's Cross Sermon of 9 February 1588/9,' *Journal of Ecclesiastical History* 20, no. 2 (1969): 253–66.

Carr, J. A. *The Life and Times of James Ussher Archbishop of Armagh*. London: Gardner, Darton, 1895.

Clay, William Keating, ed. *Liturgical Services: Liturgies and Occasional Forms of Prayer Set Forth in the Reign of Queen Elizabeth*. Cambridge: Parker Society, 1847.

Collinson, Patrick. *The Elizabethan Puritan Movement*. London: Jonathan Cape, 1967.

Cox, John E., ed. *Miscellaneous Writings and Letters of Thomas Cranmer*. Cambridge: Parker Society, 1846.

Culbertson, Eric. *The Evangelical Roots of the Church of Ireland: James Ussher and the Irish Articles*. Lisburn, Northern Ireland: CIEF, 1999.

Cust, Richard, 'The Defence of Episcopacy on the Eve of Civil War: Jeremy Taylor and the Rutland Petition of 1641,' *Journal of Ecclesiastical History* 61, no. 1 (January 2017).

Davies, Ebenezer Thomas. *Episcopacy and the Royal Supremacy in the Church of England in the XVIth Century*. Oxford: Blackwell, 1950.

Dugmore, C. W., ed. *Studies in the Reformation: Luther to Hooker*. London: Athlone Press, 1980.

Ehrman, Bart D., ed. and trans. *The Apostolic Fathers*. Loeb Classical Library. Cambridge, MA: Harvard University Press, 2003.

Elliot, Mark W., trans. *Ancient Christian Commentary on Scripture: Old Testament XI: Isaiah 40–66*. Downers Grove, IL: IVP, 2007.

Elrington, Charles, ed. *The Whole Works of the Most Rev. James Ussher, D.D., Lord Archbishop of Armagh, and primate of all Ireland. The*

Whole Works of the Most Rev. James Ussher, D.D., Lord Archbishop of Armagh, and Primate of All Ireland. 17 vols. Dublin: Hodges, Smith & Co., 1864.

Erastus, Thomas. *Explicatio gravissimæ Quæstionis, utrùm excommunicatio quatenus religionem intelligentes et amplexantes, a Sacramentorum usu, propter admissum facinus arcet, manadato nitatur Divino, an excogitata sit ab hominibus.* London: Pésclavii, 1589.

Ferguson, William. *Scotland's Relations with England: A Survey to 1707.* Edinburgh: Saltire Society, 1994

Fesko, J. V. *The Theology of the Westminster Standards.* Wheaton, IL: Crossway, 2014.

Ford, Alan. *James Ussher: Theology, History, and Politics in Early-Modern Ireland and England.* Oxford: Oxford University Press, 2007.

Ford, Coleman. '"Everywhere, Always, By All": William Perkins and James Ussher on the Constructive Use of the Fathers.' *Puritan Reformed Journal* 2 (2015).

Freedman, J. S. 'The Diffusion of the Writings of Peter Ramus in Central Europe c.1570–c.1630.' *Renaissance Quarterly* 46 (1993).

Gardiner, S. R. *Constitutional Documents of the Puritan Revolution, 1625–1660.* 3rd edition. Oxford: Clarendon Press, 1906.

Gee, Henry, and William John Hardy, eds. *Documents Illustrative of English Church History.* New York: Macmillan, 1896.

Gribben, Crawford. *The Irish Puritans: James Ussher and the Reformation of the Church.* Darlington, England: Evangelical Press, 2003.

Harford, George and Morley Stevenson, eds. *The Prayer Book Dictionary.* New York: Longmans, Green & Co., 1912.

Herberman, Charles G. et al., eds. *The Catholic Encyclopedia.* 16 vols. New York: The Encyclopedia Press, 1914.

Heylyn, Peter. *Aerius Redivivus, or, the History of the Presbyterians. Containing the Beginnings, Progresse, and Successes of that Active Sect. Their Oppositions to Monarchical and Episcopal Government. Their Innovations in the Church: and their Imbroilments of the Kingdoms and Eftares of Christendom in the pursuit of their Designs. From the Year 1537 to the Year 1647.* Oxford: n.p., 1670.

Holmes, Michael W., ed. *The Apostolic Fathers: Greek Texts and English Translations,* 3rd ed. Grand Rapids: Baker Academic, 2007.

Hooker, Richard. *The Folger Library Edition of the Works of Richard Hooker.* Edited by W. Speed Hill, 7 vols. Vols. 1–5, Cambridge, MA: Belknap Press, 1977–1990; Vol. 6, Binghamton, NY: Medieval & Renaissance Texts & Studies, 1993; Vol. 7, Tempe, AZ: Medieval & Renaissance Texts & Studies, 1998.

Kirby, Torrence, ed. *A Companion to Richard Hooker.* Leiden: Brill, 2008.

Knox, Buick. *James Ussher: Archbishop of Armagh.* Cardiff: University of Wales, 1967.

Lamont, William M. *Godly Rule: Politics & Religion.* London: Macmillan, 1969.

Lightfoot, J. B. *The Apostolic Fathers.* London: Macmillan, 1907.

Luther, Martin. *The Works of Martin Luther,* Translated by Herbert J. A. Bouman et al. Edited by J. Pelikan and H. Lehmann. 55 vols. Saint Louis, MS: Concordia, 1958–1986.

Macinnes, A. I., and Jane Ohlmeyer, eds. *The Stuart Kingdoms in the Seventeenth Century.* Dublin: Four Courts, 2002.

Marcellus of Ancrya. *The Panarion of Epiphanius of Salamis, Books II and III.* De Fide. Translated by Frank Williams. Leiden: Brill, 2013.

Maruyama, Tadataka. *The Ecclesiology of Theodore Beza: The Reform of the True Church.* Geneva: Librairie Droz, 1978.

McCrie, Thomas, and William Row, eds. *The Life of Mr Robert Blair, Minister of St. Andres, Containing his Autobiography from 1593– 1636, with Supplement to his Life, and Continuation of the History of the Times to 1680, by his Son-in-law, Mr William Row, Minister of Ceres.* Edinburgh: Woodrow Society, 1848.

MacCulloch, Diarmaid. 'Richard Hooker: Invention and Reinvention.' *Ecclesiastical Law Journal* 21 (2019).

McGiffert, Michael. 'Grace and Works: The Rise and Division of Covenant Divinity in Elizabethan Puritanism.' *Harvard Theological Review* 75 (1982).

Metzger, Bruce. *A Textual Commentary on the Greek New Testament.* 2nd ed. Stuttgart: Deutsche Bibelgesellschaft, 1994.

Milton, Anthony. *Catholic and Reformed: The Roman and Protestant Churches in English Protestant Thought, 1600–1640*. Cambridge: CUP, 1994.

Milton, John. *Complete Prose Works*, vol. 1. Edited by John Cox. New Haven: Yale University Press, 1953.

Pearson, A. F. S. *Presbyterian Origins in Ireland*. Belfast: Presbyterian Historical Society of Ireland, 1948.

Peck, Linda L., ed. *The Mental World of the Jacobean Court*. Cambridge: CUP, 1991.

Perkins, Harrison. *Catholicity and the Covenant of Works: James Ussher and the Reformed Tradition*. Oxford: OUP, 2020.

Reid, J. S. *History of the Presbyterian Church in Ireland*. New York: R. Carter & Bros, 1860.

Rogers, Thomas. *The English Creede*. London: n.p., 1587.

Schaff, Philip. *The Creeds of Christendom*, Bibliotheca symbolica ecclesiae universalis. 3 vols. New York: Harper Longmans, 1919.

Snoddy, Richard, ed. *James Ussher and a Reformed Episcopal Church: Sermons and Treatises in Ecclesiology*. Moscow, ID: Davenant Press, 2018.

Sommerville, M. R. 'Richard Hooker and his Contemporaries on Episcopacy: an Elizabethan Consensus.' *Journal of Ecclesiastical History* 35, no. 2 (1984).

Spalding, J. C. and M. F. Brass. 'Reduction of the Episcopacy as a Means to Unity in England, 1640–1662.' *Church History* 30 (1961).

Spurr, Joh, *English Puritanism 1603–1689*. New York: Palgrave Macmillan, 1998.

Stewart, A. T. Q. *The Narrow Ground: The Roots of Conflict in Ulster*. London: Faber & Faber, 1989.

The Book of Common Prayer and Administration of the Sacraments. Cambridge: Cambridge University Press, 2004.

The First and Second Prayer Books of Edward VI, Everyman's Library. London: J. M. Dent & Sons, 1910.

Travers, Walter. *A Full and Plaine Declaration of Ecclesiastical Discipline out of the Word of God* (n.p., 1574).

Trevor-Roper, Hugh. *Catholics, Anglicans and Puritans: 17th Century Essays*. Oxford: Oxford University Press, 1987.

Ussher, James. *Certain Briefe Treatises Written by Diverse Learned Men, Concerning the Ancient and Moderne Government of the Church.* Oxford: n.p., 1641.

Ussher, James. *The Reduction of Episcopacie unto the Form of Synodical Government Received in the Antient Church: Proposed as an Expedient for the compremising of the now Differences, and preventing of those Troubles that may arise about the matter of Church-Government.* London: T.N. for G.B. and T.C., 1656.

Ussher, James._Episcopal and Presbyterial government conjoyned proposed as an expedient for the compremising of the differences, and preventing of those troubles about the matter of Church.* London: [s.n.], 1679.

Wengert, Timothy J., *Priesthood, Pastors, Bishops: Public Ministry for the Reformation and Today.* Minneapolis, MN: Fortress Press, 2008.

Whitgift, John. *Works of John Whitgift.* Edited by J. Ayre. 3 vols. Cambridge: Parker Society, 1852.

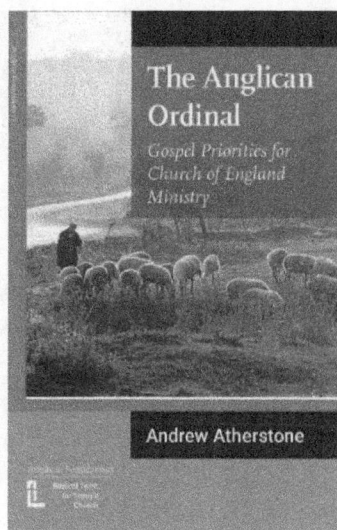

The Anglican
Ordinal

Gospel Priorities for
Church of England
Ministry

Andrew Atherstone

This book is part of our *Anglican Foundation* series, which offer practical
guidance on Church of England services.

There is no better handbook for Anglican ministry than the Anglican
ordinal – the authorized liturgy for ordaining new ministers. The ordinal
contains a beautiful, succinct description of theological priorities and
ministry models for today's Church. This booklet offers a simple
exposition of the ordinal's primary themes. Anglican clergy are called to
public ministry as messengers, sentinels, stewards, and shepherds. They
are asked searching questions and they make solemn promises. The Holy
Spirit's anointing is invoked upon their ministries, with the laying-on-of-
hands, and they are gifted a Bible as the visual symbol of their new
pastoral and preaching office. This booklet is a handy primer for
ordinands and clergy, and all those responsible for their selection,
training, and deployment.

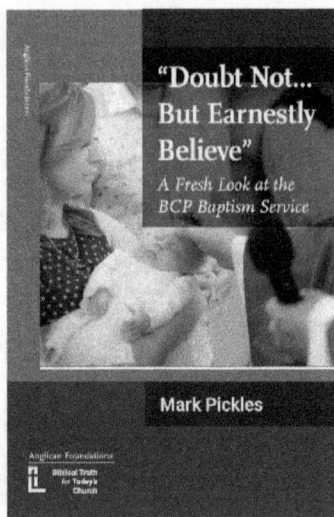

"Doubt Not... But Earnestly Believe"
A Fresh Look at the BCP Baptism Service

Mark Pickles

Whilst Common Worship (2000) provides a Book of Common Prayer Communion (BCP) in modern English, sadly there is no such provision for the BCP baptism service. For some Anglican evangelicals this may not seem to be a particularly regrettable omission.

There are those who might not be persuaded of the biblical mandate for baptising infants, whilst others might have concerns over some of the language used that may appear to affirm 'baptismal regeneration'. This booklet is an attempt not only to engage with those questions and concerns but also to proffer an enthusiastic support for the theology and liturgical content of the BCP Baptism service. It has a great emphasis on the covenantal grace of God which encourages Christian parents to "doubt not – but earnestly believe" in God's faithfulness and mercy. In so doing it directs our primary focus to our promise keeping God and not to ourselves.

To Tell the Truth

Basic Questions and Best Explanations

J. Andrew Kirk

Latimer Publications
Biblical Truth for Today's Church

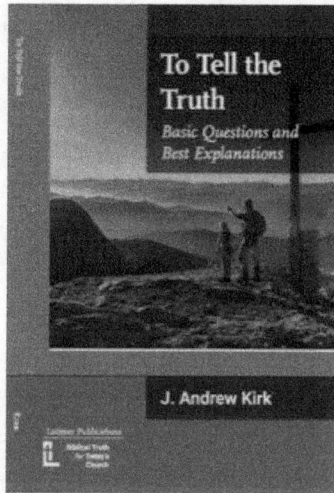

Human beings are inquisitive people. We all, quite rightly, like to explore the real world in its many fascinating dimensions. In particular, there are a few deep questions that most people face at some time in their lives: Who are we? Is there an overall purpose for our lives? What is good to believe? Why is there so much evil and suffering around? How is evil to be overcome and suffering accounted for? What best can help us to know how we should live? What is truth and how can we know it?

For well over a millennium and a half the Christian Faith has guided the Western world and, more recently, other parts of the world in how to answer these and many other questions. However, its answers have also been strongly disputed, sometimes with hostile intent. In this book, Andrew Kirk argues strongly that the Christian Faith, in spite of all that has been thrown against it, still represents by far and away the best explanations for these profound enigmas of life. Here you will find convincing answers, and reasons why alternative ideas do not ultimately match the full realities of our existence.

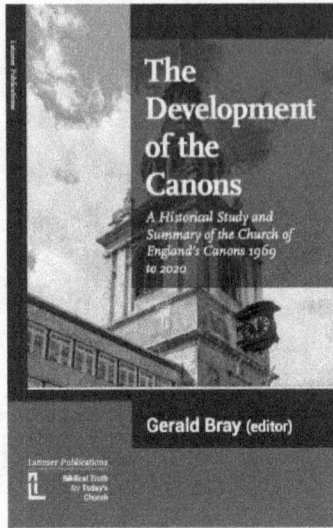

The
Development
of the
Canons

*A Historical Study and
Summary of the Church of
England's Canons 1969
to 2020*

Gerald Bray (editor)

Latimer Publications

After three and a half centuries of relative neglect, the Church of England embarked on a thoroughgoing reform of its Canons, which led to the promulgation of an entirely new series of them in 1964 and in 1969. A year later, the present General Synod was inaugurated, and since then the Church's canon law has undergone a sometimes bewildering number of additions and alterations.

Keeping track of these developments is not easy, because although the material is available, until now it has not been gathered together in one place or set out in a user-friendly format. This book is a compilation of the 1964/1969 Canons with all their many modifications in the first half-century of their existence. It has no legal authority of its own, and those wanting to know what Canons are currently in force will need to consult the official publications of the Church of England.

This edition is a reference work aimed to clarify how the Church has developed its Canons over the past fifty years. As such, it will be of great benefit to historians, and to lawmakers in the Church who want to find out what has happened to the Canons in the recent past, even as they make new ones for the future. It is a snapshot taken in 2020 that provides a template for the study of a work that is still in progress, even as it continues to reflect the principles and practices that have guided its development since 1970.

www.ingramcontent.com/pod-product-compliance
Lightning Source LLC
Chambersburg PA
CBHW021140020426
42331CB00005B/840